Mr. Terrance A. Weir
215 W. Chocolate Ave. Apt. 9 Y
Hershey, PA 17033

Mr. Terrance A. Weir
215 W. Chocolate Ave. Apt. 9 Y
Hershey, PA 17033

The Adirondacks

Mr. Terrance A. Weir
215 W. Chocolate Ave. Apt. 9 Y
Hershey, PA 17033

creating the north american landscape

Gregory Conniff
Edward K. Muller
David Schuyler
CONSULTING EDITORS

George F. Thompson
SERIES FOUNDER AND DIRECTOR

Published in cooperation with the
Center for American Places,
Santa Fe, New Mexico,
and Harrisonburg, Virginia

The Adirondacks

WILD ISLAND OF HOPE

TEXT AND PHOTOGRAPHS BY

Gary A. Randorf

THE JOHNS HOPKINS UNIVERSITY PRESS

WITH A FOREWORD BY

Bill McKibben

BALTIMORE AND LONDON

To Albert (Cap) Randorf, for introducing me to the wonders of the natural world, and to all those who have labored for the protection and preservation of the Adirondack Park and wild places everywhere.

This book was brought to publication with the generous assistance of The Adirondack Council and its grantors: Furthermore, a program of the J. M. Kaplan Fund; the Nordlys Foundation; and the Norcross Wildlife Foundation, Inc.

Published 2002
Printed in Italy on acid-free paper
9   8   7   6   5   4   3   2

The Johns Hopkins University Press
2715 North Charles Street
Baltimore, Maryland 21218-4363
www.press.jhu.edu

Library of Congress Cataloging-in Publication Data
will be found at the back of this book.

A catalog record for this book is
available from the British Library.

ISBN 0-8018-6953-6 (pbk.)

A soft, dazzling splendor filled the air. Snowy banks and drifts of cloud were floating slowly over a wide and wondrous land. Vast sweeps of forest, shining waters, mountains near and far, the deepest green and the faintest, palest blue, changing colors and glancing lights, and all so silent, so strange, so far away, that it seemed like the landscape of a dream. One almost feared to speak lest it should vanish.

HENRY J. VAN DYKE
July 1885
Harpers New Monthly

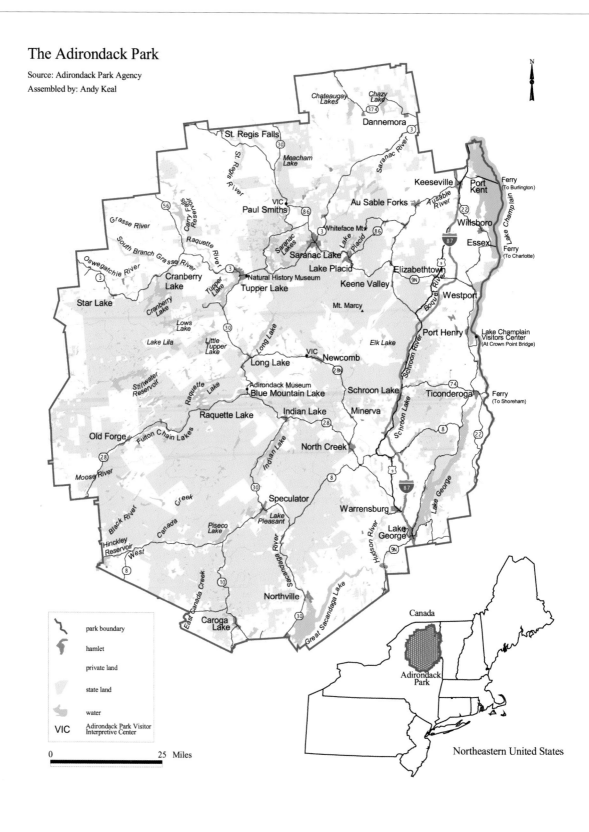

The Adirondack Park

Source: Adirondack Park Agency
Assembled by: Andy Keal

N

Chateaugay Lakes
Chazy Lake
374
Dannemora
3
St. Regis Falls
30
Meacham Lake
Saranac River
Keeseville
Port Kent
Ferry (To Burlington)
St. Regis River
VIC
Paul Smiths
86
Au Sable Forks
Ausable River
22
Willsboro
Grasse River
56
Carry Falls Reservoir
Whiteface Mt
3
Lake Placid
86
87
Essex
Raquette River
Saranac Lakes
Saranac Lake
Ferry (To Charlotte)
South Branch Grasse River
Lake Placid
Elizabethtown
9N
Oswegatchie River
3
Natural History Museum
Keene Valley
Boquet River
Cranberry Lake
Tupper Lake
Tupper Lake
Westport
Star Lake
Cranberry Lake
Mt. Marcy
Lows Lake
30
Long Lake
Elk Lake
Port Henry
Lake Champlain Visitors Center (At Crown Point Bridge)
Lake Lila
Little Tupper Lake
VIC
Newcomb
Schroon River
Stillwater Reservoir
Long Lake
28N
74
Ticonderoga
Raquette Lake
Adirondack Museum
Blue Mountain Lake
Schroon Lake
Minerva
Ferry (To Shoreham)
Raquette Lake
Indian Lake
Schroon Lake
8
22
Old Forge
Fulton Chain Lakes
28
North Creek
Moose River
Indian Lake
8
87
Creek
30
Speculator
Warrensburg
Lake George
Black River
Canada
Piseco Lake
Lake Pleasant
Hudson River
Lake George
Hinckley Reservoir
West
9N
8
Sacandaga River
10
Northville
30
East Canada Creek
Caroga Lake
Great Sacandaga Lake

Legend

- park boundary
- hamlet
- private land
- state land
- water
- **VIC** Adirondack Park Visitor Interpretive Center

0 ——————— 25 Miles

Canada
Adirondack Park
Northeastern United States

contents

foreword

I walk out the door behind my home in the southern Adirondacks and climb a steep mountain slope, beech and birch shading into spruce and pine. At the top, a small clearing lets me look west. And what is there to see? Transcendence? Splendor? Not precisely—not high rock, not sharp spire, but ridge upon rill upon low mountain, disappearing over the horizon. Here is the first lesson about the Adirondacks, captured in Gary Randorf's magnificent photos. It is not only alpine granite—in fact, of the park's 6 million acres, only about eighty-five, scattered on top of the tallest mountains, are that gorgeous pseudo-Arctic. Aside from the touristed High Peaks, the Adirondacks comprise millions upon millions of acres of Low Peaks, of beavery draws and bearish woods, of hills and hills and hills, countless drainages and muddy ponds. Americans have pretty reliably saved the rocks and ice in countless parks and wildernesses across the country, but here, through the accidents of politics and the largenesses of vision that Randorf describes, we have the setting as well as the stone. An ecosystem, a bioregion, a real place, whole and complete. Splendid in a different way, more breathtaking to consider, perhaps, than to look at. Taking one's breath away is not the point of the Adirondacks—instead, it's a place to breathe normally, fully, deeply, calmly, in a territory that looks like the world once looked.

I keep walking, down the mountain now, following a spruce-hemmed creek. There are no trails on this land, except the well-traveled and economical lines the deer walk. And yet, after about an hour, I come to a clearing. Apple trees gone native mark the edge, and in the center, under an ancient maple, is a cellar hole. Home now to a growing birch, three generations ago it was the center of a farmer's life. He cut this hole in the woods and outlined it with rock, built a home for himself and his wife, and here brought children into the world. And eventually he gave up—a growing season of ninety days and some years when the frost came every month, no easy way to get his crop out to market, work too unrelenting even for an unrelenting family. And the state bought the land, and the forest, lumbered over and pastured over and wandered over, grew back in to tracklessness. Is that sadness? In a way. But humans flourish elsewhere. The second point about the Adirondacks, a glory carefully revealed in the words and pictures of this book, is that it represents a second-chance wilderness and, as such, a hope that the damage caused by human beings is not irreversible. It is metaphor as much as place.

What else? The source of the wilderness idea, enshrined almost carelessly by the state legislature when it amended New York's constitution to keep these lands "forever wild," words that drugged Bob Marshall and then Howard Zahniser and all the rest of the gentle zealots inspired by this place.

And what else? The first, and America's only, large-scale experiment in whether or not people can manage to live in and around wilderness, whether a region can support human beings and the rest of nature without one blotting out the other. I talked not long ago with an extraordinary pair of biologists in the thick of a fight to save places like the mountain gorilla refuges of Rwanda. The emerging paradigm of conservation in developing nations—protected areas, buffer zones, land-use controls—is the paradigm of the Adirondacks, the best because longest-running experiment in whether—to put it as sharply as possible—limits are possible.

millions of years was geologic, when uplifted mountain ranges alternated with flat plains and shallow seas. Continental glaciers flowing over and sculpting the land created the landscape we see today.

Human history began with the American Indian. When the first Europeans arrived during the early seventeenth century, northern New York was part of the hunting grounds of the Mohawks, one of the Six Nations of the Iroquois. The northern reaches of what is now the Adirondack Park was disputed territory, also claimed by the Algonquins of Canada.

Forbidding to settlers, the Adirondacks remained largely unexplored until the mid–nineteenth century. The year before American independence was won, an early mapmaker wrote of the region: "This country by reason of mountains, swamps and drowned lands is impassible and uninhabited." Until Mount Marcy, New York's highest mountain, was climbed for the first time in 1837, it was believed that the highest mountains in New York were in the Catskills. Adirondack historian Alfred Donaldson observed in 1921 that Stanley had found Livingstone and told the world about the depths of Africa before most New Yorkers knew anything substantive about the wilderness in their own backyard.

While much of the earlier history of the region is well worth studying, I emphasize the last quarter-century, a period of sustained controversy, when preservationists have argued that the chance to make the area a lasting wilderness park is disappearing. At the same time some residents have felt threatened by land-use controls and regulations that are perceived as further restricting their ability to make a living in an economically depressed rural area.

I have been in the middle of the debate, having worked for the Adirondack Park Agency, the state authority with jurisdiction over the park's private lands, and the Adirondack Council, the preeminent private group dedicated to preservation of both the natural and the cultural resources of the park. The largest of only two park advocacy groups headquartered within its boundaries, the council has been the target of militant park opponents, who have vented their wrath by picketing the council several times and who have on occasion threatened council personnel with bodily harm and property damage.

The Park Agency, too, has at times been the subject of abusive behavior by park detractors. In its infancy (the agency was established in 1971), its building was pelted with rotten eggs, and arsonists just missed burning it down on October 20, 1976. Staff were regularly threatened, and tires were slashed on their state cars. In the summer of 1991, several bullets were fired at an agency automobile while three staffers (who were in the vehicle) were conducting a field inspection.

Surprising? Not really. Many expect wild places and things, open space, outdoor recreation, scenic beauty, and pure water, land, and air to be made available for their enjoyment and consumption without personal sacrifice and their own dedication to the health of the land. Their attitude seems to be, "Do what you will, government, but don't tell me what I can and cannot do with my land. I pay taxes on it, and I will do what I damn well please."

This may be an exaggeration. Most park landowners do not maintain this extremist view. I would argue that the vast majority of New Yorkers, including Adirondackers, don't want to see outside land speculators and developers carve up the private land and sprinkle condominiums and town houses far and wide. They don't want this place to change much, for they realize what they have is something special but still vulnerable to all the pressures of a new century of fast-paced growth and change. The irony and the sadness is that individuals and groups with divergent opinions have overemphasized their differences and taken too little time and effort to identify their common ground, which in my view far exceeds their differences.

The subject of this book is important because it deals with issues of land use and land-use philosophy. Unless common solutions can be found to balance natural and wilderness resource protection with appropriate and sustainable economic activity and growth, the promise of the Adirondack Park will be squandered. The ramifications will be universal and significant. It has become all too obvious that our national parks and other natural and wild areas cannot be forever protected in isolation. As often as not, their ecosystems extend beyond their neat and precise boundaries onto adjacent private lands. The many values these refuges represent—biological, natural, recreational, spiritual, economic, social, and as sources of physical and mental health—will ultimately be destroyed or hopelessly impaired if surrounding private lands are not subject to comprehensive and restrictive land-use planning and control. The issues are complex, much is at stake, and time is running out.

Laws and regulations can, to a degree, help save this park of private and public lands, but over the long haul only human caring and positive human actions can ensure its continued health and integrity. Stewardship is essential, as is the adoption of a land ethic. This book is for park residents, visitors, landowners, recreationists, politicians, business people, educators—anyone who has ever enjoyed or just cared about places natural and free. We must combine forces to carefully and wisely do everything possible to sustain the many values of the Adirondack Park and other places like it. We must make a statement individually and jointly that global concerns such as acid rain, the "greenhouse effect," ozone depletion, and human overpopulation must be met and conquered, or this park and other places like it will be irreparably damaged.

I will argue for the protection of the park's roadless, wilderness areas, its wild and scenic rivers, and its still vast open spaces. I will share with you how I enjoy the park and introduce you to its natural history because I believe that you must know and understand a place before you can be talked into saving it. And like few of my fellow park residents, I have had the opportunity to get to know these special resources, having spent almost three full years in the field walking its trails and paddling its rivers. Much of what I missed during river studies for the Adirondack Park Agency I have experienced during my own personal travels to photograph the park's back country. I spent the winter of 1987–88 ski touring more than three hundred miles of state trails to photograph and write about them for the two Visitor Interpretive Centers at Paul Smiths and Newcomb.

So I confess to feeling not only eminently qualified but also morally bound to write about these wild places, to stress their quality and rareness. They compare in beauty with what I have seen in Alaska, New Zealand, Africa, Hawaii, Iceland, Australia, Norway, and Patagonia. Here we have an opportunity, and must exercise the responsibility, to preserve the special, wild character of these places. The world is watching. We are and will continue to set an example of how to do it—that is, saving a wilderness that includes people. If we fail, we fail not only our state, our country, and ourselves, but also the world.

chapter one

Paths in the Forest

Not so many years ago, I had the opportunity to walk a lovely path through old growth forest from the vicinity of Little Moose Lake to the banks of the south branch of the Moose River. It was one of those experiences that remain indelible in my mind because the scene and the ambience were otherworldly. I felt as if I had been catapulted back in time to an earlier era. This was the forest primeval. Generously spaced, huge sugar maple and yellow birch trees rose, columnlike, straight up to a lucent green canopy, twinkling and shifting in the wind and sunlight. Below grew a lush, lacy layer of ferns and wild-flowers, which I would have had no difficulty at all traversing if I had taken off on a tangent from the well-worn path we were following. The forest was pleasantly cool. Only rarely did the sun find an opening in the roof of leaves through which to splash rays of golden light on the ancient scene before me. All the rest was in shadow, green, subdued, and transparent, as if I were peering into the dim, liquid recesses of a tropic sea.

Here, one could imagine that the scene was unchanged from centuries ago. I have had similar experiences bushwhacking to the shore of Rhododendron Pond near Keene Valley and drift boating through the Hudson River Gorge upstream of North River, where I have imagined that I was peering through the eyes of an Indian who passed this way long before the first white men saw this country.

Indian Land

There were Indian trails in the Adirondacks when the Europeans arrived. They were well-worn paths, a foot or more in width and sometimes a foot in depth, indicating that they had been routes of travel for a long time. Lake George and Lake Champlain were traveled by canoe in summer and on snowshoes in winter. There were other north-south trails. One came up the Hudson, cut through Indian Pass (in the High Peaks between Wallface and the MacIntyre Range), and approached the Plains of Abraham near Lake Placid. Trails then led to Lake Champlain and north to the Saint Lawrence River. Another trail, today a popular canoe route, ran down the Fulton Chain of Lakes and the Raquette River, then through Coreys via Stony Creek Ponds to Indian Carry on Upper Saranac Lake, and then overland to Lake Champlain. Still other trails ran through the depressions or valleys that surround northern New York.

Whether the makers of these trails (the Mohawks, one of the Iroquois Nations, and the Algonquins, a Canadian tribe), who both laid claim to the Adirondacks, ever settled in the region is open to debate. Evidence seems to indicate that they did, however, since Indian village sites have been uncovered at Chazy and Cranberry Lake. Additionally, axlike tools have been found along the Saranac River and Saranac

Lake, and pottery shards have been recovered near the Saint Regis River, along with a bowl at Silver Lake.

Prevailing theory suggests that as early as 8000 B.C. there were wanderings into New York State of small groups of Indian hunters equipped with chipped-stone tools. It is believed that they were descendants of a population that had spread into North America via a land bridge at the Bering Strait some 7,000 to 12,000 years earlier. It seems entirely feasible that Indians were at least penetrating into the valleys and lowlands surrounding the Adirondacks within a few centuries after the last glaciation, 10,000 to 12,000 years ago. This last glaciation left us with the landforms we see today. It rounded off mountains that were once much higher, carved out valleys, and backed

Lake Champlain and the Adirondacks from Vermont

up waters in numerous lakes and ponds as moraines blocked the great glacial rivers that resulted from the enormous runoff of surface waters. It is helpful to picture the Adirondack region as a vast elevated plateau that rises into lofty mountain summits in the interior but slopes gradually down on every side into valleys and plains. In the valleys run the water courses that begin in the high country, emptying off the plateau like spokes of a wheel.

The Iroquois and the Algonquins were a hunting and fishing people who also practiced agriculture. The flint-tipped arrow and spear were the primary hunting weapons. Most fishing was done with nets, clubs, spears and harpoons, and bone gorges (straight pieces of bone hidden in a mass of bait and then engorged by the fish).

Most of Algonquin culture was organized around a quest for food that followed the cycle of the seasons. After the autumn harvest of berries, nuts, edible roots, and other natural crops, the people scattered in extended families to fish and hunt in the winter. Spring brought larger numbers together again at the fish runs and sugar maple groves. Villages formed to enjoy the bounty of summer, when some gardening was done.

As a dwelling, the wigwam was well adapted to the needs of traveling people. For hunters pursuing large game animals, it was relatively easy to move the structure of poles and bark, mats, or skins to the food supply. Animal furs and leather provided clothes, blankets, and furnishings for the lodge. Trees provided a wide range of life's necessities. Twine was made from twisting narrow strips of bark. Splints of bark were woven into boxes and baskets. Arrow shafts, spoons, bowls, pipes, and paddles were also made from nearby trees. Equally useful was bone for the making of awls, needles, scrapers, and arrow points.

Pervading the Algonquin philosophy was the ethic of respect for the environment and compassion for all living things. From the abundance of creation, nothing was to be taken unless it was truly needed. People, fish, birds, and animals were part of a brotherhood. Wildlife shared an equal part of creation with humans. The essence of wildness was a tonic for the soul that was to be preserved for future generations.

The Iroquois, too, saw the presence of the Creator in all life. Nature was recognized as the embodied spirit of the Creator's thoughts of beauty for this world. Before and after social events, the Iroquois expressed their thankfulness for the profusion of life and nature in a Thanksgiving Address. With such respect they were to make use of their surroundings without abusing mother earth, the source of supply.

Sometime between the middle of the fifteenth and of the sixteenth centuries, an inspired Huron mystic, Deganawidah, brought a message of hope and goodwill to the woodland tribes of upstate New York. "Put aside petty feuds," he told them, "and form a new brotherhood based upon law and order." Within five years Deganawidah's first convert and chief disciple, Hiawatha (not to be confused with Longfellow's romantic hero) had formed a wilderness confederacy. The Indians called it the Great Peace; to the white man it was the League of Iroquois. The Five Nations forming the confederacy were the Seneca, Oneida, Onondaga, Cayuga, and Mohawk. There was also a branch of the Iroquois in the Carolinas, the Tuscaroras, who united with the Five Na-

West Mill Brook,
Dix Mountain Wilderness

Pine woods at Gabriels

tions in 1715, after which the confederacy was known as the Six Nations. The Indians of the Five Nations were a practical people. Corn, beans, and squash, the "three sisters," formed the staple of their diet, with venison and fish in season. When not attending the crops, women and children gathered wild produce such as acorns, beechnuts, butternuts, chestnuts, and hickory nuts. Particularly popular were strawberries, raspberries, blueberries, and cranberries. Maple sap was collected in spring for the preparation of syrup and sugar.

Contrary to common belief, the league was not a military alliance. In fact, the league ruled by power of mind rather than by force of arms. The Iroquois were powerful out of all proportion to their numbers because they were able to manage complex alliances based on persuasive visions of reality shared by large numbers of people. They were great orators given to articulate expression of ideas. Though surrounded by potential enemies, they not only survived but prospered. Out of Onondaga, capital of the confederacy, decisions that affected the continent were made.

When the Europeans first arrived on the shores of North America, they lacked the skills of survival. They did not know how to raise corn or to hunt turkeys and other game, and they were unprepared for winter. The Indians taught them the skills of survival. The Europeans also

From Gothics Mountain

Lake George from Tongue Mountain

Connery Pond near Lake Placid

learned from the Indian mind. So much of Indian thought found its way into the European mind that the revolution of thought that separates the medieval world from the modern world can be traced to some extent to the interaction between Europeans and the natives of America.

The league is most valued for the ethics upon which it was based and the democratic beginnings that came from its institutions. The league provided for a classless society in which women were equal with men, chiefs were servants of the people, and decisions were reached by consensus. The Iroquois League had a direct influence on the later development of democratic government in both Canada and the United States. Benjamin Franklin and Thomas Jefferson freely acknowledged their debt to Iroquois principles when drawing up the beginnings of America's federal republic and Bill of Rights. The social organization of the Iroquois Peace League compares with the present-day United Nations and stands as a notable achievement in the record of institutions of peace. When Deganawidah, the Peacemaker, stood before the first gathering of the united Iroquois nations at Onondaga, he planted a Tree of Great Peace as a symbol that was to give power and permanence to their union. The Great White Pine, which pierces the sky and reaches to the sun, signified the law, that is, the constitution, which expressed the terms of their union. The branches signified the shelter, protection, and security of their uniting together. The roots, which stretched to the four quarters of the earth, signified the extension of the law, the peace, to embrace all humankind. Other nations, not yet league members, would see these roots as they grew outward, and if they were people of goodwill, would follow them to their source and take shelter with others under the tree.

During the opening ceremonies of the Adirondack Park Visitor Interpretive Center at Paul Smiths in the spring of 1989, Iroquoian Jake Swamp planted a pine tree near the main entrance to the Interpretive

I've made hundreds of ferry crossings of Lake Champlain and have also plied its notably attractive waters by canoe and sailboat. On some of these trips, I've tried to imagine what it was like for Samuel de Champlain when, as the first white man to do so, he entered the "wilderness sea of the Iroquois" after an arduous passage up the rapids of the Richelieu River in July 1609 and laid eyes on the Adirondacks. Champlain was impressed with "a number of beautiful islands filled with fine woods and prairies." Crystal clear waters spread southward to the horizon. From thickly wooded shores on either side rose verdant foothills, and distant ranges of mountains were visible. It must have been a most exciting prospect. Champlain was accompanied by two companions and a party of Hurons, Algonquins, and Montagnais Indians. They traveled in a couple of dozen canoes, proceeding cautiously up the lake only by night and resting on the shore by day, for they were in the land of the Iroquois, arch rivals of the Algonquin nations.

Near the head of the lake, Champlain and his party met a band of Iroquois and a fight ensued. Champlain advanced to the front with harquebus in hand, clad in the metallic armor of the day. While the Iroquois warriors stood gazing in astonishment at this strange, warlike apparition, Champlain leveled his harquebus and fired, instantly killing two Iroquois. That shot set the stage of history for the next 150 years. The Iroquois became friends and allies of the English, while the Algonquins aligned themselves with the French. This first encounter in the forested fringes of the Adirondacks was the forerunner of a long and bloody warfare between the French and English and their respective Indian allies, and the soil of the Adirondacks often formed the battleground.

FACING PAGE
Clear Pond from Grandpa Pete Mountain

Although a few Jesuit missionaries trod the Lake Champlain–Lake George route, along with trappers from Montreal and Fort Orange (later Albany), only a handful of whites settled on the fringes of the Adirondacks in the eighteenth century. In 1779, New York State passed an "Act of Attainder." That statute said in essence that the United States had won the Revolutionary War and that all lands owned by those loyal to the Crown were now its spoils. New York State laid claim to most of the lands north of the Mohawk River, somewhere between 7 million and 12 million acres. Thereafter, New York State tried desperately to get rid of that land by passing a series of statutes like "an Act to promote the expedient settlement of the waste and unappropriated lands of the State." The state set up "military tracts," bounty lands for Revolutionary War soldiers. Apparently there were very few takers, and the Adirondacks remained little explored until the 1830s, when tourism began and small factories appeared on the fringes. Explorers had discovered the sources of the Columbia River sixty years before the northernmost source of the Hudson was finally located by Verplanck Colvin in 1872. Mount Washington, the highest mountain in New Hampshire, had been climbed almost two hundred years before geologist Ebenezer Emmons, artist Charles Ingham, and a small party of scientists made the first ascent of what proved to be the highest mountain in New York in the summer of 1837. Emmons named the surrounding peaks the Adirondacks, and he named Mount Marcy in honor of the governor.

Several economic themes run through Adirondack history. Although the area has had its share of newcomers seeking to make their fortunes, not many have made it big. Descendants of New England settlers came to make a living by farming the rocky soil. They soon recognized the mountains as the hardscrabble area they are and retreated into the surrounding valley fringes. Others sought fortunes mining

East branch of the Ausable River,
Adirondack Mountain Reserve, Saint Huberts

iron ore. Magnetite is the principal source of Adirondack iron ore, and there were rich deposits in many locations, including the Port Henry/ Mineville area, at Tahawus near Newcomb, at Lyon Mountain, and near Star Lake. Until the late 1800s the Adirondacks supplied much of the iron used in the eastern states. This industry is defunct today because of the expense of building roads and dams, and the problem of impurities in the ore always made iron ore production risky at best. The primary impurity turned out to be ilmenite, eventually found to be processible into titanium dioxide. It was used during World War II for smoke screens and other wartime materials. Titanium dioxide, because of its extreme whiteness, was until relatively recent times produced at Tahawus as a pigment for the finest paints. But today all is quiet at Tahawus.

Another white material, wollastonite, has been mined at Willsboro and more recently at Lewis. Its primary use is as an ingredient in

From the slopes of Giant Mountain

West branch of the Ausable River, North Elba

At Lake Lila

industrial and decorative ceramics. Its value increased dramatically about a decade ago when it was found to be a nontoxic substitute for asbestos. Garnet has been mined near North Creek since 1878. Most garnet mined today is used industrially for sandpaper, emery boards, and other abrasive products.

Others tried to strike it rich from the great supply of lumber, fur, and hides. By 1845 there were fifteen hundred tanneries and seven thousand sawmills spread over much of the Adirondacks. Lumbermen reached the center of the woods in 1850, when New York State led the nation in timber production. New York no longer leads the nation in timber production, but the industry still ranks second only to tourism in the Adirondacks. Over 1 million acres of private park land are owned and managed by timber product companies.

The discovery and ever widening use of the region as a vacation land has been the brightest star in the Adirondack economy. Tourism began in the 1830s but catered then only to the rich. From 1845 to

Clear Pond from Macomb Mountain

1875, the wilderness became available to many. There were popular accounts, especially in William H. H. Murray's *Adventures in the Wilderness* (1869), of fish jumping into boats and deer wandering into gun sights, of a wonderland of riches all there for the taking. Murray's books were handed out with train tickets, causing a "stampede to the woods." Those who were lured to the Adirondacks and found more mosquitoes and blackflies than fish or game were called "Murray's fools." Currier and Ives were reproducing A. F. Tait paintings of the sporting life in the Adirondacks in the mid-1800s, and about the same time the profession of guiding arose and a new round of hotel building took place on the Saranac Lakes, at Lake Placid, Paul Smiths, Long Lake, Blue Mountain Lake, Keene, Schroon Lake, and Lake George.

To transport city-bred "sports" (hunters, fishermen, campers), a professional guide needed a suitable boat, since lakes and rivers served as the only roads at the time. After trying the Indian canoe and finding it lacking, the unique Adirondack guide boat was developed. These fast, low, sleek, wooden boats are still skimming Adirondack waterways after more than a century. The guide boat is "a canoe built like a row boat," as some have described it. The credit for fashioning the first one usually goes to the guide Mitchell Sabattis. The boat's ribs are cut from naturally shaped spruce roots. The thin but strong planking is made of pine or cedar. After the sawing, beveling, and fitting, the planking is fastened to the ribs with brass screws and the joints are nailed with copper tacks. The heads of the five thousand tacks and three thousand screws help decorate those boats that are finished with several coats of varnish. They are storm-worthy boats and can carry four and even six people across a choppy mountain lake in a storm. "Don't worry none in this boat," one guide used to say, "You're as safe in it as you are in the Lord's pocket."

Along with the hunters and fishermen who penetrated the wilderness in the 1870s came the wealthy of the Eastern establishment, including such families as the Morgans, Vanderbilts, Whitneys,

On the summit of Cascade Mountain

From Weston Mountain,
Hurricane Primitive Area

Lehmans, Harrimans, and Rockefellers. On their large private tracts encompassing lakes, rivers, and woods, they built rustic yet elaborate "great camps." Great camp builders created a vernacular style that was later to be emulated in the hotels of the Pacific Cascades, the Rockies, and the Great Lakes, as well as in National Park Service buildings across America. The structures combined a mixture of logs, native stone, and decorative rustic work of twigs, branches, and bark. The camps were usually multiroomed, rambling affairs with luxurious lay-outs of large dining and living rooms and numerous bedrooms to ac-commodate the owners and an array of guests. Often there was a com-plex of buildings that included guest cottages, separate retreats for fa-vored family members, caretaker and staff houses, boat houses, storage sheds, and farm buildings. Sometimes there were chapels and even bowling alleys.

The owners might stay a few months, weeks, or only a few days in the year. Arriving for the summer at a typical great camp on Upper Saint Regis Lake took some doing, as William Chapman White de-scribes in *Adirondack Country* (1954):

Anson Phelps Stokes, wife, seven children, one niece, about ten servants, Miss Rondell, one coachman, three horses, two dogs, one carriage, five large baskets of tents, three cases of wine, two packages of stove pipe, two stoves, one iron pot, four washstands, one barrel of hardwood, four bundles of poles, seventeen cots and seventeen mattresses, four canvas packages, one buck board, five barrels, one half barrel, two tubs of butter, one bag coffee, one chest tea, one crate china, twelve rugs, four milkcans, two drawing boards, twenty-five trunks, thirteen small boxes, one boat, one hamper.

Some great camps remain today as private retreats, conference centers, and inns. During the summer months Camp Sagamore near Raquette Lake, owned by the Sagamore Institute, offers informative tours of the camp and its surroundings and information about the great camps generally.

The Adirondacks has hosted its share of notable literary figures and artists. The soaring mountains, the wilderness with its vast retreats and silences, and the remote lakes and ponds have provided inspiration and quiet places to think, write, and paint. Few places have been written about more prolifically and by a wider variety of authors, including James Fenimore Cooper, John Burroughs, William James, Robert Louis Stevenson, Theodore Dreiser, Joyce Carol Oates, and E. L. Doctorow. Artists of the Hudson River School, such as Thomas Cole and Frederick Church, were followed by Winslow Homer, Frederick Remington, Rockwell Kent, Georgia O'Keeffe, John Marin, Harold Weston, and many present-day painters, including Frank Owen, Allen Blagden, Patricia Reynolds, Ellen Phelan, Don Nice, Paul Matthews, Ann Pember, Anne Lacy, Don Wynn, and Linda Fisher.

There were several philosophers' camps in the Adirondacks, the most famous being the encampment at Follensby Pond, south of the Saranacs, in the summer of 1858. Here Ralph Waldo Emerson, James Russell Lowell, Louis Agassiz, and a group of other distinguished in-

Saint Huberts from Hopkins Mountain

tellectuals gathered to espouse the goodness of nature and of men living close to it. Longfellow had been invited but, after hearing that Emerson was going to take a gun, he refused lest someone be shot. More recently, the centennial year of the Adirondack Park in 1992 was celebrated by events including a re-creation of the first philosophers' camp, with present-day thinkers including author Bill McKibben.

The early photographer, Seneca Ray Stoddard, was stimulated by both the Adirondack wilderness and the people and their culture. In recent times Eliot Porter, David Muench, George Wuerthner, Carr Clifton, and Nathan Farb have made photographic images of the Adirondack landscape that have received wide national exposure.

Painter Harold Weston, in *Freedom in the Wilds* (1971), wrote eloquently of the artistic inspiration these mountains provide:

Unnamed brook, Dix Mountain Wilderness

As we reached the top [of Basin Mountain] and looked toward Johns Brook suddenly there was a glimpse of autumn trees blazing in sunlight in the valley below us. A bit later in almost the opposite direction the cold shoulder of Haystack emerged from the clouds and a moment later to the left of it Boreas Ponds silvery and shimmering. It was tantalizing because the vision was wiped away before you could grasp it all. The tempo of the moving clouds calmed down after a while and it cleared as we watched the movement of sun patches and shadows sweep up and over the bare glistening slides of the western ridge of Gothics, with Giant in the distance now benignly warming up in the steady sunlight. I did four paintings in a frenzy. The wild exuberance of the day and its successive orgasms of wilderness beauty called for a shorthand method in paint to capture rapidly changing emotional reaction, methods that predated abstract expressionism. It was indeed a morning of glory.

There are many spots of historical and cultural interest in the Adirondacks. History buffs and sightseers are drawn to the very attractive restored fort and grounds at Ticonderoga, where Benedict Arnold assembled the first American fleet in 1776. Nearby is Crown Point (1759), with the preserved remains of Fort Saint Frederic (1734), along with a visitor center that houses historical and archeological exhibits. Lake George was the site of many early battles, and the Americans scored a decisive pivotal victory over the British at Plattsburgh during the War of 1812.

The ideal place to gain an overall perspective on the history and culture of the Adirondacks is the Adirondack Museum in Blue Mountain Lake. In a beautiful setting, its handsome buildings house a fascinating array of collections and exhibits that are unrivaled by any other regional historical museum in America.

chapter two

A Forest Forever

Treadway Mountain sits in the heart of the Pharaoh Lake Wilderness, a 46,000-acre tract east of Schroon Lake that is part of the more than 2.8 million acres of publicly owned and constitutionally protected Adirondack Forest Preserve. Looking south from Treadway's summit, one sees unbroken forests encircling Pharaoh Lake, an extremely attractive body of water that is wholly within the Pharaoh Lake Wilderness. In fact, when you turn on your heel on Treadway's rocky apex, an almost trackless woods rolls away in all directions. From the top of Pharaoh Mountain, it is the same story—woods sprawling to the horizon whichever way you turn.

You can enter the Pharaoh Lake Wilderness from the north near Paradox or Eagle Lake, from the east near Chilson, or from the south near Adirondack. But from whatever point you choose, you hike

From Weston Mountain near Keene

through miles of dense woods that are broken only by ponds, streams, and wetlands. This is but one of dozens of vast tracts of Forest Preserve where the woods are not only continuous but also untouched by human hands. Hike into the Giant Mountain Wilderness from route 9 near New Russia, and you will encounter miles and miles of hemlock stands, hardwood forests, mixed woods, and pure stands of white birch before reaching the crest of Rocky Peak Ridge and the summit of Giant Mountain. Head into the Hoffman Notch Wilderness on its north side from the Blue Ridge Road, and you will be pleasantly relieved as you leave the first mile of cutover, managed private forest land and enter the natural, wild, and uninterrupted woods of the Forest Preserve. Someday all of the preserve's woodlands will likely resemble a forest primeval. At least they will remain in their unbroken grandeur because New York State's constitution declares that they remain "forever wild."

It wasn't always this way.

Exploiting the Wilderness

> *The New World was like a blank piece of paper on which*
> *men might write the outlines of a better world, a world in*
> *which the mistakes of the past were not to be repeated*
> *and perpetuated ... The red men did not fit into these*
> *plans. They were unfortunate intruders on the dream,*
> *and so they were pushed back, shunted outside the dream*
> *and when occasionally they rebelled at being shoved out*
> *of the way, the brutal wars broke out ... The land was*
> *free and it belonged to those who took and subdued it.*
> *Men were no longer serfs or peasants or bonded men;*
> *they owned land, thousands of acres of land. It was*
> *theirs to do with what they wished.*
>
> —JEAN RIKHOFF, *Buttes Landing*

The first chopping down of the Adirondack woods began shortly after the English replaced the Dutch as the landlords of New Netherlands and changed its name to the Province of New York. Early on, the Crown adopted a policy of granting vast tracts of land to those in the good graces of the ruling family. With little thought to the future, the grantees began a wholesale harvest of the timber resources. The logging operations generated wealth for the owner and removed the cover that provided a haven for Indians. Logging also opened up the valley land for early farming. Throughout colonial times, the higher mountains remained largely untouched while the valleys were transformed by logging, potashing, and land clearing.

The logging industry was the worst offender in despoiling Adirondack forests. Clear-cutting and the fires that often followed laid waste to the land. Steeper terrain, now barren, was eroded, and streams that had before run year-round dried up in summer. The trees and their root systems, which had acted like a giant sponge, were gone. Buying the land cheap from the original speculators, the lumbermen stripped the great primeval forest and let the ruins revert to the state in lieu of paying taxes.

View from Mount Marcy

Businesses other than lumbering further impoverished the forests. The tanning industry depleted the hemlock until most tanneries were forced out of business because of lack of hemlock bark. The paper industry consumed the spruce and fir. The charcoal industry thrived on clear-cutting as it devoured wood of all sizes and shapes. As a result of the charcoal burners' operations, a forest might be totally stripped of all growing stock. The iron industry consumed vast supplies of charcoal for the operation of kilns to process the ore. Farmers sometimes girdled or more often burned trees to clear the land for farming, their only use for wood in that case being as ashes to mingle with soil as fertilizer. Farmers even cleared lands on mountain slopes that they soon realized were unsuitable for farming or grazing.

The game and fish of the Adirondack region were treated with sim-

On Cascade Mountain

Off Owls Head, Keene

mutton" that could be found. The vast harvest was sold to game deal-
ers, who supplied hotels and restaurants in downstate cities. Lumber
camps and thriving local hotels provided additional markets.

The prized fish found by the settlers of the Adirondacks were the
speckled or brook trout and the large lake trout. Some of the rivers
were full of salmon. The fish were there for the taking; there were no
limits or seasons. By the mid–nineteenth century, stories of the extraordinary fishing caught the attention of a public that was paying
more and more attention to life outdoors. At first the goal was big fish,
but that soon degenerated to fish of any size. The trout and salmon
went fast. There were stories of catching 120 pounds of trout in a couple of hours. "Fished out" became a common cry.

The First Visionaries

By 1850 the wilderness was rapidly changing and in some cases disappearing. About all that remained untouched were the inaccessible
peaks and passes. Fortunately, a few people noticed what was happen-
ing. Among the first to be concerned was Joel T. Headley. Though most
of his book, *The Adirondack; or, Life in the Woods* (1849), was a romantic account of the glories of the Adirondacks and nature, Headley
expressed some alarm about "a new state of things": "New highways
cut the forest, hunters' boarding houses have sprung up along the lake
shores . . . where I once roamed alone with my companions, I must now
expect to meet white tents and ladies and gentlemen from every part
of the country. . . . A little of this is pleasant, but the wilderness without solitude loses half its charm for me, and I am resolved to strike off
to some point where no sights or sounds shall meet me to remind me
of the outer world."

In 1864, a *New York Times* editorial suggested that concerned citizens should band together and, "seizing upon the choicest of Adirondack Mountains, before they are despoiled of their forests, make of

them grand parks, owned in common." In that same year George Perkins Marsh's book, *Man and Nature*, was published. Described by some as the "fountainhead of the conservation movement," it was the first great book on ecology. Marsh had studied forests and their watersheds in many parts of the world. He argued that the indiscriminate cutting that occurred on a grand scale in the Adirondacks in the nineteenth century was "the most destructive among the many causes of physical deterioration of the earth." The woods, with their dense root systems, trap moisture in the soil, ensuring the "permanence and regularity of natural springs, not only within the limits of the wood, but at some distance beyond their borders, and thus contribute to the supply of an element essential to both vegetable and animal life."

Norman VanValkenburgh, in his short history, *The Forest Preserve of New York State in the Adirondack and Catskill Mountains* (1983), says that "the writers of these statements were the 'urgers,' what was needed were some 'doers.' In 1865 they showed up." Franklin B. Hough was a country doctor from Lewis County on the western fringe of the Adirondacks and a historian. In 1865 he supervised the state census and traveled extensively in the Adirondack region gathering data. The condition of the forests enraged him. As a self-taught forester he was aware of the dire results that could occur if the destruction of the watershed forests were to continue. He called for the adoption of forest conservation practices and used his influence with friends in government to arouse public sentiment on this matter.

Also in 1865, Verplanck Colvin, a young man of eighteen, made his first journey to the Adirondack wilderness. He had prepared a map showing the land grants of the Adirondacks and decided to visit the area to check out his work. He followed a route along the Sacandaga River to a point near Speculator. He was amazed at "the natural park-

FACING PAGE

Flume Fall, near Wilmington

like beauty of this wilderness." Colvin climbed Mount Seward in the Western High Peaks region in October 1870, after camping with his guide the night before on the upper slopes. He wrote that "the view was magnificent, yet differing from other of the loftier Adirondacks, in that no clearings were discernible, wilderness everywhere, lake on lake, river on river, mountain on mountain, numberless." Colvin wrote a report of the climb and submitted it to the New York State Museum of Natural History. He stressed the need for preservation of the forests to assure a future water supply for the state and recommended to the museum and the state legislature that an "Adirondack Park or timber preserve" be established.

In 1872 the legislature appointed Colvin as chief of the Adirondack Topographical Survey and made him a commissioner of state parks, along with Franklin Hough. The commission's first report to the legislature in 1873 called for the immediate protection of "a great portion of that Forest from wanton destruction." Colvin worked tirelessly in the following years, charting and chronicling the wilderness with scores of guides, surveyors, axmen, and packers. By horse and wagon and by boat, his expeditions and the reports they engendered focused attention on the exploitation of the mountains and called for the protection that the exploitation increasingly demanded. As Verplanck Colvin wrote in 1874:

Unless the region be preserved essentially in its present wilderness condition, the ruthless burning and destruction of the forest will slowly, year after year, creep onward after the lumbermen, and vast areas of naked rock, arid sand and gravel will alone remain to receive the bounty of clouds—unable to retain it . . . and the streams that now are icy cold in the shadows of the dark, damp woods will flow exposed to the sun, heated and impure . . . The dense forest . . . prevents evaporation. In spring, moreover, it shields the accumulated snow of winter from the sun's direct rays, and prevents it from rushing suddenly off in furious floods.

From Hopkins Mountain

The lumbermen pushed farther into virgin headwater forests. Dam builders, storing water to flush logs downstream and to generate power, were drowning lush, verdant river valleys and critical wildlife habitat.

A Forest Preserve

In 1885 the recommendations of Colvin and Hough finally took form when the State Parks Commission, headed by Charles Sargent, recommended in their report that a forest preserve be established in the Adirondacks. Sargent was the foremost tree expert in the United States and the founder of the Arnold Arboretum in Boston. The commission noted the advantages of a continuing forest for the flow of water and as a natural recreational area to be enjoyed by the people. It laid the blame for the destruction of the forests on the lumbering and charcoal

Gill Brook, Adirondack Mountain Reserve, Saint Huberts

industries and on the construction of numerous reservoirs throughout the mountains.

On May 15, 1885, the Forest Preserve became a reality as the state legislature embodied the Parks Commission's recommendations into law and established a three-man Forest Commission to protect the preserve from trespass, fire, and further plundering. The Adirondack Forest Preserve was defined to be all the lands "now owned or which may hereafter be acquired by the State of New York" within eleven Adirondack area counties (Oneida County was added later in 1887) and further provided that "the lands now or hereafter constituting the Forest Preserve shall be forever kept as wild Forest lands. They shall not be sold, nor shall they be leased or taken by any corporation, public or private." When the statute went into effect, the state was the owner of 681,374 acres in the Adirondacks.

An Adirondack Park

The establishment of the Forest Preserve was a giant step in the preservation and protection of Adirondack forests. But a law is only as good as its administration, and any law can be changed by the passage of another. Opponents of preservation looked for ways to ease restrictions. In 1887 they managed to get a law passed that empowered the Forest Commission to sell "separate small parcels or tracts wholly detached from the main portion of the Forest Preserve." The commission interpreted the word *small* very liberally and contracted to sell off parcels as large as more than thirty-five hundred acres. The commission also began to urge in its annual reports that laws be passed to allow lumbering on all parts of the preserve. The public became concerned. Verplanck Colvin became incensed. Colvin had continued his survey of the Adirondacks. He repeatedly suggested in his annual reports to the legislature that a park should be established in the High Peaks region and that all lands in this area should be acquired by the state as a preservation forest. Largely through Colvin's persistence, a 2,800,000-acre Adirondack Park was established by the legislature on May 20, 1892.

The boundary of the park was indicated on the map as the now famous "Blue Line." The law did little other than to designate an area within which to concentrate land purchases by the state. To the chagrin of those striving to achieve true protection of the Adirondacks, the park law permitted the Forest Commission to sell state lands anywhere in the Adirondacks and to lease state lands within the park for private camps and cottages. The interests of those opposed to preservation were still being favored.

Constitutional Protection

By 1894, the preservationists and the general public had reached the limit of their patience. They found a way to achieve meaningful and lasting protection of the Forest Preserve at a constitutional convention convened that year. Included in the proposed new constitution was a covenant to preserve in perpetuity what was left of the forests. Henceforth the trees of the Adirondack Forest Preserve would be held as "forever wild" as the lands and waters. As David McClure said during the convention:

There is no necessity why we should part with any of our land. We should not sell a tree or a branch of one. Some people may think in the wisdom of their scientific investigations that you can make the forests better by thinning out and selling to lumbermen some of the trees. But I tell you no man has yet found it possible to improve upon the ways of nature . . . The hills, rock-ribbed and ancient as the sun—the venerable woods—rivers that move in majesty—and the complaining brooks that make the meadows green, these for years had been neglected by the people of the state . . . the men of public spirit generally, had forgotten that it was necessary for the life, the health, the safety, and the comfort not to speak of the luxury of the people of this State, that the forests should be preserved.

In a show of accord that has probably never been repeated in any matter relating to the Adirondacks, the convention approved the "forever wild" clause by a vote of 112–0. The clause became part of a new constitution that was approved in November 1894 by a vote of 410,697–327,402. The clause read: "The lands of the state, now owned or hereafter acquired, constituting the Forest Preserve as now fixed by law, shall be forever kept as wild forest lands. They shall not be leased, sold or exchanged, or be taken by any corporation, public or private, nor shall the timber thereon be sold, removed or destroyed." New York

Red maple and birch

now had the toughest and most permanent means of protecting wild lands of any state in the nation. And it still does.

Continuing Vision

The "watershed argument" (i.e., the argument that the woods function as a fountain, releasing a continuous supply of water) was cited as the primary reason for preserving the forests, despite the fact that the benefit of a Forest Preserve as a "great resort for the people of the state" was noted during the constitutional convention. Only later did people begin to see the great value of the preserve for wilderness recreation and as an ecological and scenic reserve. Defending the Forest Preserve became the goal of many citizens. Over the years they have grouped together to make their opinions heard. As T. Morris Longstreth wrote in *The Adirondacks* (1917):

Indeed, if Hough, Colvin, The Association for the Preservation of the Adirondacks, a succession of public-spirited governors, and tireless groups of incorruptible persons had not labored for a generation, there would have been no great

Unnamed tributary of Styles Brook, near Keene

On Crane Mountain, Johnsburg

North Woods for future Americans to enjoy . . . only by herculean efforts on the part of the few, was a succession of bills prevented from passing the legislature, which would have permitted companies to dam most of the valley land at public expense for private profit . . . For years the State had been acquiring and holding lands, often denuded, to be sure, which lumber interests did not pay the taxes on. It was this nucleus of property that gave the idea for the Park. Curiously enough, in this way, avarice was its own undoing . . . In 1885 the Forest Preserve was created, and the popular vote in 1894 set it aside for the use of all the people forever.

The Adirondack Park has been enlarged several times. In 1912 a new law extended the Blue Line to follow tract and lot lines that more nearly conformed to the outside limits of the so-called Great Forest of Northern New York. The law also defined the Adirondack Park as "all lands located within the following described boundaries"—thus including, for the first time, private land in the park designation. The park's size jumped to 4,054,000 acres.

In 1916 the first bond issue for the acquisition of Forest Preserve was approved by the voters to provide $7,500,000 for the purchase of lands to be added to both the Adirondack and Catskill Forest Preserves. By the time the funds were expended in 1927, the Adirondack Forest Preserve totaled 1,917,063 acres. The new acquisitions focused primarily on the High Peaks region of Essex County and the headwaters of the Oswegatchie River in Saint Lawrence County.

In 1931 the Adirondack Park was enlarged to a total of 5,600,000 acres, with the boundary being extended on all sides: easterly to Lake Champlain, southerly to the Sacandaga Reservoir, westerly to Oneida County, and northerly to the mountainous area beyond Lake Placid. In 1956 the park's Blue Line was extended to add an additional 100,000 acres to the northeast corner. Finally, in 1972, the Blue Line was pushed out again on the east to the center of Lake Champlain and on the northeast to include Valcour Island and additional areas in Clinton and Franklin Counties. Essex County now joined Hamilton County wholly within the Blue Line.

In eighty years the Adirondack Park more than doubled in size from its original 2.8 million acres to almost 6 million acres. From 1885 to the present, the Adirondack Forest Preserve (the public land owned by all New Yorkers) has grown from 681,000 acres to 2,800,000 acres, over four times larger than at its inception. The Adirondack Park includes both the publicly owned Forest Preserve lands and all privately owned lands within the Blue Line. In other words, the nearby-to-me, 4,000-acre Forest Preserve Split Rock Mountain tract is park land, but so too is my 70-acre farm. The public and private lands added together make up the 6-million-acre park.

Probably no one in this century fought harder and more effectively for the protection of the Forest Preserve than did John Apperson. Apperson was a bachelor, enthusiastic hiker, sportsman, and engineer

Looking into Dix Mountain Wilderness from Giant Mountain Wilderness

who specialized in patents for the General Electric Company in Schenectady. John was originally a Virginian; he came to the Adirondacks early in the twentieth century to view a canoe race and fell in love with the mountains. His favorite area was the southern fringe at Lake George. When the state began to move squatters from the Forest Preserve in 1915, it was aided in the task by Apperson, who made the removal of camps on the Lake George Islands one of his personal missions. He was less dismayed than were state personnel by some of the squatters' political connections. "Lake George is my wife," Apperson once said, "and its islands are my children." Apperson did not confine his efforts to Lake George alone, however. He fought for state acquisition of pristine lakes, mountaintops, and other scenic and vulnerable areas, and he rallied his followers to do battle with any forces that threatened the integrity of the Adirondack Park's wilderness.

Efforts to diminish the park have regularly been mounted but have been unsuccessful. Of more than 150 proposed amendments to the "forever wild" article in New York's constitution, only a few have been approved. State voters and their elected representatives have resisted major changes. In 1911, the people were asked: Shall it be proper to use 3 percent of the Forest Preserve for water supply reservoirs? The people said, Yes. In 1922: Shall it be proper to develop the preserve for hydroelectric power? The people said, No. In 1932: How about closed cabins and other recreational facilities in the preserve with the necessary clearings of timber? No, said the people. In 1940: Shall we construct ski trails on Whiteface Mountain that will be eighty feet wide? Yes, said the people. In 1958: Surrender three hundred acres for construction of I-87, the Northway? Yes, said the people, though barely. In 1967: Should we relax to some degree the forever wild provision, so that some land might be put to "better use"? And the people said, No, we should not.

Legal interpretation of the "forever wild" provision has been strong and clear. Said Judge Harold Hinman in a landmark case considering the proposal to build a bobsled run on Forest Preserve land for the 1932 Olympics:

Giving [it] the significance which the term "wild forest" bears, we must conclude that the idea intended was a health resort and playground with the attributes of a wild forest park as distinguished from other parks so common in our civilization. We must preserve it in its wild state, its trees, its rocks, its streams. It was to be a great resort for the free use of the people in which nature is given free rein. Its use for health and pleasure must not be inconsistent with its preservation as forest lands in a wild state. It must always retain the character of a wilderness. Hunting, fishing, tramping, mountain climbing, snowshoeing, skiing, or skating find ideal setting in nature's wilderness. It is essentially a quiet and healthful retreat from the turmoils and artificialities of a busy urban life.

In the 1940s a battle erupted over free-flowing rivers in the Adirondack Park. Pressure mounted to build dams and reservoirs on the south branch of the Moose River. Dams at Higley and Panther Mountains would have flooded the Forest Preserve. Led by Paul Schaefer, the preservationists swung into action. Schaefer's Moose River Committee rallied thousands of citizens in opposition to the dam proposals. The governor's help was called upon, with Schaefer delivering an eloquent plea:

A citizen may not have title to his home, but he does have an undivided deed to this Adirondack land of solitude and peace and tranquility. To him belong the sparkling lakes tucked away in the deep woods and the cold, pure rivers which thread like quicksilver through lush mountain valleys. His determination to preserve his personal treasure for posterity has been tempered by memories of campfires, and strengthened by pack-laden tramps along wilderness trails and by mountaintop views of his chosen land. To him the South Branch of the Moose is a River of Opportunity, for he has come to regard it as the front line of defense against the commercial invasion of his Forest Preserve.

Birches, "pioneers" of the forest

In 1953, the decade-long battle was over. The voters of New York State approved a constitutional amendment banning reservoirs in the Forest Preserve.

Fine-tuning

The "forever wild" provision in the state constitution started a never-ending argument over forest use, which is still being waged in the post offices, taverns, general stores, and barbershops of the Adirondacks. But in the state woods things were quiet after 1894. The scars of logging and fire began to heal. Timber trespass subsided.

In the early decades of the 1900s, however, recreation in the Forest Preserve increased dramatically. The state cut and marked hiking trails and built the first developed campgrounds. As more people came and demanded conveniences, the State Conservation Department (renamed the Department of Environmental Conservation in 1970) responded by building more facilities in the state woods. They erected boat docks on shorelines, along with tent platforms, fireplaces, and privies. The department built lean-tos, and eventually clusters of them were constructed. They put fire towers on the mountaintops. Telephone and electrical lines followed. More years passed, and then the department penetrated the preserve with roads, jeep trails, and fire truck trails. And in recent times, they added helicopter platforms and snowmobile trails. Students of the preserve began to be concerned that the department was overdoing the building of facilities and was "domesticating" the woods.

With the opening of the Adirondack Northway in the mid-1960s, that other part of the Adirondacks—the private lands—came under attack, for there was hardly a land-use control on the books in all of the Adirondacks. The Adirondack Park was now within an easy drive of millions of metropolitan New Yorkers and the adjacent urbanites of Connecticut and New Jersey. They, along with the millions of other people within a day's drive of the park, with their increased leisure time and expanding incomes, began discovering these mountains as a prime place to acquire a summer residence or wilderness acreage.

And so it was reasoned in the summer of 1967 by Laurance Rockefeller, chairman of the State Council of Parks and brother of then-Governor Nelson Rockefeller, that the only way to save the Adirondacks was to make of it a 1.7-million-acre Adirondack Mountains National Park. It was expected that preservationists and other outdoor enthusiasts would relish such a proposal. Instead, there was an almost unanimous protest from all interest groups and park supporters. Concern over the fate of the remaining millions of acres; over what would happen to private inholdings, which even included villages; and over the loss of hunting rights and the recognition that national park status could never afford the measures of protection provided by the state caused the demise of the proposal before it got off the ground.

Brainchild of a study commission appointed by Governor Rockefeller, the Adirondack Park Agency (APA) was established in 1971 and in the following two years devised two major master plans for the park.

The first classified the state Forest Preserve lands into five main categories based upon their characteristics and capacity to withstand use. The most strictly controlled lands, which total more than 1 million acres, are designated as Wilderness, Primitive, and Canoe Areas. They are maintained as primeval, where primitive types of nonmotorized recreation are permitted, including hiking, fishing, hunting, cross-country skiing, and canoeing. Many of the structures and facilities that the Conservation Department had been sprinkling throughout the preserve, such as fire towers and observer cabins, boat docks, storage sheds, roads, and jeep and snowmobile trails, were phased out and considered nonconforming. More than 1 million acres of additional preserve lands were classified as Wild Forest. A higher degree of human use is allowed, including motorized access in designated areas. finally, Intensive Use Areas, though limited in acreage, permit more concentrated human use as boat-launching sites, campgrounds, and beaches.

The second plan devised by the APA is the Adirondack Park Land Use and Development Plan, which guides growth and development on the park's private lands. A complicated plan, it is designed to control development, not thwart it, by funneling growth into and around existing hamlets that have roads, services, and utilities. Private holdings are divided into six categories ranging from Hamlet to Resource Management, each with its own guidelines for density of development and compatible uses.

With these two plans the Adirondack Park was on its way to being a park in more than name only. The agency paid particular attention to limiting development and growth in areas containing or adjacent to the park's fragile natural resources.

FACING PAGE
Rainbow Falls, Adirondack Mountain Reserve, Saint Huberts

Wilderness

It is easy to dream the wildest of dreams while sitting on the granite shelves of rock on Lake Lila's shore in the west central Adirondacks, for the wild scene here has changed little since the forests first reclaimed the landscape after the last glacier retreated twelve to fourteen thousand years ago. Tall pines rise as sentinels above the heavily forested eastern shoreline. The low mountains on the western shore show no signs of timbering, at least in recent times. The water is clean and pure, and there is no telltale flotsam and jetsam of civilization. Loons sound off at any hour, joined by coyotes and owls at night. Motorboats are not allowed here. On occasion, though, when it is still, you may hear paddles and oars break the water's surface and the happy grunts of those who wield them.

My first stay on Lake Lila was mystical. We camped on Spruce Island. There are four islands that have single campsites. If you're fortunate enough to find one of these available, you are usually assured of having the whole island to yourself. I awoke slightly after sunrise that first morning and found the lake shrouded with fog clouds that were occasionally pierced by a muted, low-horizoned sun. I ran back to the tent for my camera and daypack, planning to head off in the canoe by myself to try to capture the dramatic light. My partner was now awake and was determined not to miss the show. So we set off on calm water for the round bay at the southeast corner of the lake. The fog and the

sun were in a fast dance together. For fleeting moments pines or coni-
cal cedars would appear on the shore, or we'd catch a glimpse of a
flotilla of ducks on the water. Then the fog would envelop everything,
and we'd lose all sense of where we were. Occasionally we'd hear the
laughlike cry of a loon or two. We eventually worked our way slowly
through some reed banks on the far shore of the bay and paddled into
Shingle Shanty Brook, scaring up a flock of ducks and a pair of loons,
which startled and thrilled us as they disappeared into the mist. I felt
as if we were paddling into an Oriental scroll painting.

Lake Lila, formerly a state Primitive Area, was early in 2000 re-
classified to Wilderness. The eastern portion, including the entirety of
the lake, is part of the William C. Whitney Wilderness, itself newly
classified in early 2000. To the south and west are three additional
Wilderness Areas (Pepperbox, Pigeon Lake, and Five Ponds), the latter which now encompasses the western portion of the Lake Lila tract.
The private lands nearby are largely undeveloped retreats; some produce timber as well. Some people, including this author and the
Adirondack Council, have a dream—a wild, wilderness dream. It en-
visions a 400,000-acre wilderness with Lake Lila almost at its heart. It
would be called the Bob Marshall–Oswegatchie Great Wilderness. It
won't happen quickly because there are about two dozen landowners
who own almost 165,000 acres of private land, and they aren't jumping at the chance to sell. And they won't be forced to. Even when they
are ready to sell, there remains the question of whether the state will
have the money and the will to buy. But someday it could happen, and
that's what wild dreams are made of. In the interim, it is hoped that
the landowners will continue to be the good stewards that they have
been and that they will consider the possibility of more formalized
land protection schemes, such as conservation easements, wherein
they would relinquish all or most of their development rights for mon-
etary gain, tax benefits, and the knowledge that their lands would always be protected. The dream can be kept alive if the lands aren't de-

an unbroken wilderness. Occasionally my reveries ended in a terrible depression, and I would imagine that I had been born a century too late for genuine excitement."

The Marshalls owned a camp on Lower Saranac Lake in the Adirondacks, at which Bob spent his first twenty-one summers. From his point of view, the wilderness surrounding Knollwood meant delight, not boredom. He jumped at the chance to explore the mountains and, in the company of his brother George and the family guide, Herb Clark, climbed all the surrounding peaks higher than four thousand feet.

Wilderness preservation figured prominently in Marshall's youth. His father, Louis, a renowned constitutional lawyer, frequently brought his legal talents to the defense of the Adirondack Forest Preserve. As a delegate to the constitutional convention of 1894, Louis Marshall supported David McClure's amendment to require that state-owned forest lands in the Adirondack and Catskill Mountains remain wild forever. Louis became, by his own recollection, "most active in formulating the amendment and in securing for it what was practically a unanimous vote of the members of the convention." In 1915, when Bob was fourteen, New York held another constitutional convention. Louis Marshall fought successfully to retain the "forever wild" clause.

Bob Marshall's interest in wilderness and its preservation continued to develop as he set out for more Adirondack wilds during the summers between his college years. Camping in undisturbed forest near Cranberry Lake made him philosophical: "It was pleasant, as we layed down, to reflect that we were in the heart of a tract of virgin timber about 40 miles square, absolutely unmarred by man. And yet, we could not help regretting that there should be so very few such tracts left, due to almost criminal lack of foresight of our legislatures of the nineteenth century."

While attending the New York State College of Forestry at Syracuse,

East Trail, Pitchoff Mountain, Sentinel Wilderness

Bob wrote a class paper about wilderness preservation in the Adirondacks in which he stated that the residents of New York needed a wilderness to offset the commotion of urban conditions. He went on to argue that, even if forestry practices were such that they did not disrupt the basic ecology of the Adirondacks, aesthetic and inspirational values would be destroyed. The Adirondacks, because of their beauty, ruggedness, and close proximity to a huge urban population, were uniquely suited to nonutilitarian uses. The need for such places was only going to increase.

Several years later, on July 15, 1932, Bob Marshall set out at 3:30 in the morning to see how many Adirondack peaks he could climb in one day. Around one o'clock in the afternoon, he reached the summit of Mount Marcy. There he met a young house builder named Paul Schaefer, who was a devoted conservationist in his off-work hours. Schaefer was photographing both natural beauty and human destruction in the Adirondack Park. As Marshall sat down to eat his lunch, Schaefer began telling him about some recent threats to the wild Adirondacks. He warned of a movement to allow cabins to be built in the Forest Preserve. Schaefer pointed toward Mount Adams, noting that loggers were stripping it of virgin spruce, clear to the top (Mt. Adams was and remains private land).

Schaefer's comments disturbed Marshall. Marshall said, "They promised us there would be no more cutting above 2,500 feet elevation. Those are the most critical watershed forests in the Adirondacks." Marshall paced around the summit, visibly upset. He had seen the same kind of whittling away in the wild lands of Montana, Colorado, Washington, and Oregon—wherever there was still any back country left to be whittled. Now he was convinced that some kind of nationwide wilderness organization was badly needed. "We simply must band together," he finally said to Schaefer, "all of us who love wilderness. We must fight together—wherever and whenever wilderness is attacked." Marshall followed up on his commitment to organize a national network of wilderness defenders. In 1935 he and seven others formed the Wilderness Society, dedicated to "battle uncompromisingly" for wilderness protection all over the country.

Bob Marshall belongs in the Adirondack record because it was in the Adirondacks that he first recognized the need for wilderness preservation, an idea that he shared with others in places far and wide. Bob Marshall's efforts and leadership would eventually influence the fate of millions of acres of wild land from the Great Smoky Mountains to the Olympic Peninsula. One could argue comfortably that Robert Marshall was responsible for the preservation of more wilderness than was any individual in history. And he began his quest in the Adirondacks.

Wild Rivers

In any river of the Adirondacks I see the rivers I've known all over the United States and the great brawling ones of the north as far as the Arctic tundras. When I hear the stream, when I see placid pools and the widening circles of a rising trout or hear the lonely song of a white throat at dusk, I am content and strongly fulfilled, for mine is the blood and the sinew of ancestral man, and within me are memories of forbears who for countless millennia watched and listened before me. Rivers were part of their lives. They were the highways. Here they hunted and fished, built shelters, and in the glow of campfires had visions and dreams.

The Adirondacks with their magnificent mountain complexes are interlaced by the network of living rivers that shaped them and carved their valleys, rivers as much a part of them as their eroded cliffs and ledges. Only if they are included in the great concept of keeping the Adirondacks "Forever Wild," can these beautiful mountains fulfill their destiny as refuges for the spirit of man.

—SIGURD OLSON
brochure introducing the film *Of Rivers and Men*

The Adirondack Park's wilderness exists not only on the land but also on the waters. New York State has a system of Wild, Scenic, and Recreational Rivers. Included in the system are more than twelve hundred miles of Adirondack rivers and streams. The intent of the law creating the system is to ensure that some rivers in the Adirondack Park and elsewhere in the state will remain natural and free flowing.

In the early years of the Adirondack Park Agency (1972–75), I had the good fortune to join seasoned Forest Preserve specialist, Clarence Petty, in field studies of some twelve hundred miles of Adirondack rivers. The studies involved an inventory of physical, biological, and man-made features. Our typical day in the field began in early morning at the agency's Ray Brook, New York, office as we tied down our

On Rocky Peak Ridge, Giant Mountain Wilderness

canoe on our Jeep Wagoneer. On the day described below, as reported by Dick Beamish from our field notes in an article in New York State's *The Conservationist* (February–March 1975), our objective was the west branch of the Oswegatchie in the far west of the Adirondack Park:

Arrive at access point at 9 A.M. . . . put in at bridge crossing at Mile 7 [the river has been divided into segments of one mile on the U.S. Geological Survey map to facilitate data collection] . . . paddle upstream to shallow, rocky stretch . . . commence dragging canoe through shallows, then carry canoe along trailless river bank . . . at Mile 6 stop to fill out data sheet for previous mile . . . note that section was 95 percent stillwater with several beaver dams and 5 percent shallow rapids . . . lumber road fords stream at 6.1 miles . . . snowmobile bridge/foot trail parallels south bank . . . land uses include lumbering, hunting, fishing, trapping, snowmobiling, hiking . . . snowmobile bridge crossing at 6.2 miles . . . flood plain from ⅛ to ¼ mile wide giving way to rolling hills . . . bank vegetation predominantly marsh grass, alder, spirea . . . black cherry, tamarack and spruce moving away from river . . . sugar maple, yellow birch and beech beyond . . . at 6.7 miles sight stand of white pine 75–100 years old to 30 inches diameter . . . deer tracks observed on sand bar and fresh beaver cutting frequent . . . muskrat seen swimming 100 feet ahead of canoe . . . great blue heron and spotted sandpipers noted . . . streambed consists of sand and silt in stillwater section, cobbles in rapid section . . . water cold enough for trout, clear but tea colored from decaying vegetation in beaver flows. [Data sheet now includes artistic red trickle from fresh black fly bite on writer's hand.]

Mile 6 to 5 is 70 percent canoeable with remainder all drag and carry . . . afternoon hot, sweaty, sunny, a wonderful day for insects . . . river narrows so that canoeing no longer possible . . . start bushwhacking at 5.3 miles along steep south side of river because north side impassable marsh . . . flies thicker than ever from beating through bushes. At Mile 2 river now swampy on both sides, difficult to find stream, not feasible to proceed . . . decision made to fly final 2 miles later, recording data from low altitude. Reverse process and bushwhack back to canoe, reach jeep at 4:40 P.M. . . . continue to 7.3 miles to photograph waterfall previously identified on aerial photo . . . note carpet of bunchberry dogwood flowers by trail to falls . . . back to jeep to drive to Carthage (nearest village) to spend night prior to completing West Branch from 7.3 to 13.1 miles at park boundary on following day.

In the Adirondack Park, rules ensure that the river corridors (land along both banks) receive protection against adverse development beyond that of shorelines in the remainder of the park. The difference in the three categories—Wild, Scenic, Recreational—relates to the degree of motorized access and use and the allowable development. Wild rivers and their corridors can be best described as linear wilderness areas, where there is no public road access. No new structures or other developments are permitted. They are wild and free flowing, accessible only by canoe or other nonmotorized watercraft, on foot, or by horse. Most of these stretches flow through Forest Preserve lands classified Wilderness. Only nineteen miles involve private lands in their corridors, and these are devoted to forestry or agriculture. So, for the most part these waters and the surrounding country are managed by Mother Nature. Wild Rivers receive the highest level of protection to keep them in their wild condition and are so managed. There are 155 miles of Wild Rivers in the Adirondack Park, and they include parts of the Cedar, Cold, Hudson, Indian, Kunjamuk, Opalescent, main and middle branches of the Oswegatchie, and east and west branches of the Sacandaga Rivers and Piseco Lake outlet, the West Canada Creek and its south branch, and Ouluska Pass Brook.

Scenic Rivers and adjoining lands can accommodate limited development in their corridors and occasional public road access and crossing. Most stretches are in or border Forest Preserve or flow through lands where forestry or agriculture is practiced. They are free of diversions or impoundments except for log dams. They are managed so as to preserve or restore their natural and scenic qualities. Although

Chapel Pond, Saint Huberts

regulations affecting private lands are less restrictive than those for Wild Rivers, no motorboats or aircraft can be used on Scenic Rivers, with the exception of the Marion River, the Raquette between Raquette Falls and Trombley Landing, the Elm Lake section of the Kunjamuk River, the Bog River from the confluence with Round Lake outlet to Tupper Lake, and all ponds and lakes exceeding fifty acres in surface area that are part of a river and are accessible by road. There are 517 miles of Scenic Rivers.

Recreational Rivers and their corridors can be readily accessible by public road and can accommodate a significant degree of development. The rivers may have been dammed in the past. Motorboats are commonly in use. Their corridors are managed to preserve and restore both scenic and recreational qualities. No new structures are permitted within 150 feet of mean high water except lean-tos, docks, boat houses, fences, poles, bridges, and stream improvement structures. Where single-family homes are permitted along the shore of a Recreational River, there are minimum lot widths as well as minimum setbacks for structures. The lot widths and setbacks vary with the agency's land-use categories. There are 566 miles of Recreational Rivers.

Information on how to find and experience some of these natural, free-flowing rivers is provided in chapter 3. Maps available from the Adirondack Park Agency and the Adirondack Council indicate the location and classification of all of these river segments.

During the past two centuries, many rivers in America have been dammed, developed, and polluted beyond recognition. A surprising number of Adirondack rivers have survived more or less intact. They possess notable natural qualities, offering incomparable opportunities for fishing, photographing, canoeing, kayaking, camping, riverbank dreaming, and other pastimes. Without adequate safeguards against inappropriate development, these fragile and vulnerable resources could lose forever the pristine qualities that now distinguish them: the deep trout pool below a waterfall, the stretch of still water favored by ducks and other waterfowl, the dancing rapids that quicken the pulse of paddlers, and the vista of forested hillsides across a bordering marsh.

Gliding silently by canoe along a pristine river as it meanders through colonnades of pine and balsam or pondering frenzied white water shooting rocky chasms or leaping free-falling cascades can help us develop a river's ethic. This ethic should be based upon knowledge of the total river resource. In the park's Rivers System, we can explore their beginnings in high sphagnum-lined seeps and in trickles out of rock crevices and find the relationship between clouds, trees, and soil. Decades hence we can know that those who follow in our footsteps and wakes will experience the exhilaration that only wild and free rivers can provide.

Perhaps the best reason to preserve Wilderness Areas and Wild

Rivers is because they are there and represent an increasingly rare landscape that should be available to all people now living and yet to be born, whether they be experienced as a reality or simply as an idea. Wilderness is humankind's supreme example of restraint, for it defies the ability, desire, and tendency of civilization to modify, harness, and control the earth. What a wonderful sense of humility it inspires.

chapter three

A Sense of the Place

I knew little about the Adirondacks when I was offered a job to work for the Adirondack Park Agency (APA) in the autumn of 1971. I had been to the Adirondacks a few times before and had gathered some limited first impressions—long, hard winter deep freezes, with snow bank-to-snow bank snowmobiles, and a spring darkened by swarms of blackflies. Summer would bring an overload of tourists, and fall would be beautiful if the rain ever stopped and the clouds lifted, which would be rarely. Besides, it was "redneck" country.

So each time he called for eight months, I told George Davis, the Park Agency's first planning director, that I was really not interested in leaving the pleasant Cornell campus of Ithaca, New York, to move to New York's "Siberia." Thank God, he persisted. I reluctantly was interviewed at APA headquarters in April 1972. Here was an opportunity to do the field work for which I had prepared myself in graduate school. A few weeks later I reported to work as a natural resources planner.

On my third day on the job, Davis asked me to join seasoned biologist Greenleaf Chase (Greenie), also an APA staffer, on a field investigation of a proposed development on Upper Saranac Lake. Spring was bursting. The whole of the Adirondacks, the great North Woods, looked like they had been washed and hung out on a line to dry. Everything sparkled. Warblers and other migrating birds decorated every tree branch. We found a ruffed grouse nest containing exactly a dozen eggs. Wildflowers carpeted the forest floor. The lake was of the deepest blue, and the wavelets disintegrated on the shore like melting pieces of crystal.

I asked Greenie, "What have I done to deserve a job like this in a natural paradise?" He kindly responded, "You're just the perfect guy for it." So began my love affair with the Adirondack woods. If, after completing graduate school, someone had asked me to design the ideal job for myself, I don't believe I could have done as well. I have spent countless work days on the road or in the field photographing, documenting, and writing about this extraordinary place or at public meetings and hearings, talking about it or testifying on its behalf.

Weekends brought more discoveries. I began hiking to the mountain summits and paddling the lakes, ponds, and rivers. More recently, I have biked many of the backwoods roads. My friend Favor Smith, an Adirondack native whom I had met in college, called me up during my first August and told me about a cross-country ski sale. He wisely suggested that I get down there and buy me a pair; it would be a long, hard winter if I didn't take up playing in the snow. I thought him insane but complied. Winter is now one of my favorite seasons. By early autumn, I am already thinking about that first glide through the hills.

Blackflies are an occasional annoyance, but bug dope allows me to enter the woods even in the worst of times. And no spring is more

Dug Mountain Area, near Speculator

Fields of Essex, Champlain Valley

delightful and appreciated than an Adirondack spring if you have endured an Adirondack winter. Though mud season can be tedious, the occasional balmy breezes and encouraging signs like the return of red-winged blackbirds, the sighting of the first wildflower, the swelling of tree buds, and the honking of returning geese are enough to make cabin fever a fleeting memory.

As for the hordes of tourists in summer, we can rejoice in the fact that the Adirondack Park is large enough to accommodate all of us. With a little initiative and ingenuity, one easily can find hundreds of places off the beaten path.

There is no place more brightly gemmed than the Adirondacks in autumn. Every year the color is impressive; some years are just better than others. The sun *will* come out, and when it does it leaves you breathless. Fifty percent of the tree cover in the 6 million acres of the Adirondacks is northern hardwoods—sugar maple, yellow birch, and American beech. These are the species that turn brilliant reds, oranges, yellows, and every shade between.

As for the Adirondacks being "redneck" country, I have come to realize that entertaining the term or other such generalizing labels like "elitists" or "nature lovers" serves only to cloud the issues and to pit people of various persuasions and interests against each other. Suffice it to say that the vast majority of people who live in or use the Adirondacks wish to see the area retain its special character and quality. We just labor for its future in different ways.

For the last thirty years, then, I have spent the vast majority of my weekends and a significant percentage of my working life exploring the Adirondack Park from one end to the other. It feels like all of this Adirondack country is my community, my backyard. And yet the park is so large that there is much of it that I will never get to see. In *The Living Wilderness* (1965), Paul Schaefer articulated this vastness: "Even a lifetime will not suffice to thoroughly explore these North Woods. In forty-five years of such adventuring I find myself having a good understanding of this fact and little more—little more, that is except a deep and abiding love for the Adirondacks, a devotion which increases as the years roll swiftly onward and it becomes apparent that there are many wonderful places that, for want of time, I shall never get to see. And even in this thought there is a certain richness—!"

So there will always be for me, and for everyone, new territory to experience. I have my list of must-get-to places—Metcalf Lake, Camel's Hump and Niagara Mountains, Panther and Couchsachraga Peaks, Cold River, Winnebago Pond, and Slip Mountain, to name a few. There are also favorite places to which I return, and with the passage of time they appear as new. The Adirondacks seem to hold what William James called an "imperishable freshness." I go back where I started and get to "know the place for the first time."

Let me share with you what I have discovered in the woods, waters, and mountains of the Adirondacks. There are several ways to get an overview, where you can begin to get "a sense of the place." One way is to charter a scenic flight out of the Lake Placid or Saranac Lake Air-

Barred owl

Young moose, a species returning

ports. There are also other flying services along the Fulton Chain Lakes in the southwestern Adirondacks and at Long Lake.

But you may see almost as much if you head for some of the high spots to which you can drive your car. One such place, ironically, is Vermont: from the top of Mount Philo in Mount Philo State Park, just south of Charlotte, off route 7. Much of Lake Champlain, the High Peaks Region, and the Adirondacks beyond is seen from some rock ledges, just a short stroll from the parking lot.

In the Adirondacks there are two spectacular overviews. One is reached by driving up Prospect Mountain out of Lake George Village. From the summit you see a good stretch of the more than thirty-mile-long Lake George and an almost uncountable number of mountains, including the High Peaks, way off to the north. Another view is gained by driving up the Whiteface Memorial Highway out of Wilmington. Once to the parking lot, you can take a short hike up the rocky summit or ride an elevator to its top. A few steps from the elevator door is a vista of Lake Placid and the High Peaks that has few rivals. If you want to work a little harder for a rewarding overview, head for the Keese Mill Road out of Paul Smiths and follow the signs to the parking lot at the base of Saint Regis Mountain. It's about a 2.5-mile hike to the open rock at the top. A vast sweep of forest and waters can be seen in many directions. In the distance to the east are Whiteface, Moose, and McKenzie Mountains. Closer in one sees the Saint Regis Canoe Area and portions of the Saranac and Saint Regis Lakes.

Once you've gotten the overview, I expect and hope you'll want to see and experience more. The woods, waters, and mountains of the Adirondacks are highly accessible; those on the publicly owned Forest Preserve with rare exception offer free admission. And remember that the woods on the preserve are not managed or cut. They are as nature decides they should be.

Woods

Mountains and lakes may mark the region as unusual,
but it is the woods, above all, that makes the Adirondacks.
—WILLIAM CHAPMAN WHITE
Adirondack Country

In 1950 author William Chapman White moved to the Adirondacks. In a letter to a friend, he wrote, "Forty feet from my study the woods start and run unbroken for ninety miles." These woods are still relatively unbroken, as they are in many sections of the Adirondack Park. In fact, the park is heavily forested in all subregions other than the Champlain Valley. The vast, intact woods is what sets the Adirondacks apart from the rest of the northeast. If you hike to the summits of Vermont's Green Mountains, for instance, you realize that they make up a rather narrow, linear wilderness whose woods are rendered piecemeal by roads, farms, and villages as soon as the valley floors are reached.

The significance of the huge Adirondack woods and their inhabitants (including people) extends far beyond New York State. The area's designation, along with Vermont's portion of the Lake Champlain Watershed, as an International Biosphere Reserve by the United Na-

Wadhams Meadow

Showy lady's-slipper

Mallard

tions Educational, Scientific and Cultural Organization (UNESCO) recognizes its worldwide ecological significance and unique resource value. Presently the largest of the forty-five such reserves in the United States, the New York–Vermont Reserve is also the fourth largest in the world. The Adirondack woods are home to 90 percent of all the plant and animal species found in the Northeast. These big woods offer what few places east of the Mississippi can: vast sweeps of wilderness, where solitude and primitive recreation abound; high quality wildlife habitat that harbors diverse and unique species; almost unlimited opportunities for a broad array of outdoor recreation; the opportunity to live within a wilderness park; large and unconfined open spaces; and freedom from pollution by noise and artificial light.

A readily accessible mature forest can be enjoyed by hiking the trails of the Adirondack Park Visitor Interpretive Center at Newcomb. On the Peninsula Trail you'll see large-diameter white pine and lovely stands of hemlock and white cedar. The very attractive and undeveloped Rich Lake surrounds the peninsula, and you'll catch many rewarding views of it. Another trail crosses the lake's outlet, which is a major feeder stream of the Hudson River.

Another place to experience big trees in a handsome setting is to hike the West River Trail on the Ausable Club's Adirondack Mountain Reserve. The public is guaranteed access here by a state-held easement. You can explore to your heart's content. But, please, no camping, fishing, or hunting. And dogs are not allowed. You will see large-diameter hardwoods and conifers, along with numerous views of the east branch of the Ausable River, a Scenic River in the Wild, Scenic, and Recreational Rivers System. If I were God, this is the kind of river I'd make. It races over rocks, tumbles down numerous waterfalls, and shoots through narrow gorges. If you are up for the 3½-mile hike to the Lower Ausable Lake, you'll also see impressive waterfalls on tributary streams before reaching this rather amazing lake nestled at the base of fiordlike cliffs.

Dandelions, a rioting exotic, Westport

Wandering around in the Five Ponds Wilderness Area near Cranberry Lake is yet another good place to experience the Adirondack woods. But you'll need a lot more time to penetrate this remote area. The Adirondacks have more virgin forest than any other region in the Northeast, estimated at somewhere between 80,000 and 200,000 acres, and the largest contiguous block of uncut forest, some 40,000 acres, is found in this Wilderness Area. You can hike into the Wilderness from Wanakena or paddle into it up the Oswegatchie River from Inlet (not to be confused with the hamlet of Inlet near Old Forge), just a spot on the river accessible by a short gravel road that runs south of route 3 between Cranberry Lake and Star Lake.

The forests vary from pole-sized hardwoods in the sections that were heavily logged and burned about a half-century ago to virgin pine and spruce on the esker above the Five Ponds. On the trail to Five Ponds from the Oswegatchie, you pass through a stand of old-growth northern hardwoods before reaching Big Five, Little Five, Big Shallow, Little Shallow, and Washbowl Ponds. Another stand of original growth white pine can be found far upstream along the Oswegatchie, on the trail between High Falls and Nicks Pond, at Pine Ridge. This land was privately owned back in the days when softwood logs were floated down the Oswegatchie to sawmills. It was impractical to haul the huge logs by horse and oxen from the Five Ponds area to the landing on Wolf Creek. The big trees were spared the loggers' axes.

Interspersed with the dense forests of this Wilderness Area are numerous brooks, wetlands, and ponds. High Falls, Cat Mountain, the Plains of Oswegatchie, and, of course, the Oswegatchie River (eminently paddleable and fishable) are additional attractions, making this an area of great and varied interest. As Paul Jamieson wrote in *Adirondack Pilgrimage* (1986):

From Cat Mountain you look down on sprawling Cranberry Lake and its tentacles to the north. To the south stretches a great forest dotted with glittering ponds

. . . The variety of its topography and mystery of its forest cover can be experienced fully only by a tramper. It is a country of glacial ridges and small peaks and of innumerable brooks, lakes and ponds. Sometimes the tramper finds himself on the spine of a narrow ridge. More often the trail runs through a long glen between parallel hogbacks. Around him are hoary maples, beech, yellow birch, hemlocks, and an occasional gnarled black cherry. On the ridges above may be a row of soaring white pines outlined against the sky. A brightness in the gloomy aisle ahead may mean a beaver meadow or a pond. The sudden brilliance turns the shaggy forest into a park.

Since the mid-1980s this fascinating country has been accessible from the east via foot trails from Big Deer Pond and Lows Lake after a half-day or more paddle from a put-in point on the Bog River, near Horseshoe Lake. Primitive camping opportunities are unlimited, and at least one overnight is necessary to get into the heart of this wild territory. One of the wildest areas of the Adirondacks can be experienced by traveling southward from High Falls to Stillwater Reservoir over vestiges of the Red Horse–Oswegatchie trails, constructed by the Conservation Department about 1920 and abandoned in the late 1920s. But 5.5 miles at the south end, from Trout Pond to Clear Lake, are still maintained. You need to be an experienced back-country traveler to attempt this journey, since the northern 8 miles or so are a bushwhack. For a good guide to this trip, refer to the section "Postscript for Pathfinders" in Paul Jamieson's *Adirondack Canoe Waters: North Flow* (pp. 28–30 in 1981 edition, pp. 29–31 in 1988 edition).

Waters

The high-pitched yowls and yelps of coyotes and the eerie, laughlike cry of loons surrounded us the first night we canoe-camped on Bog River flow (also called Lows Lake) in 1986. It was the first weekend the area was open to the public, the state having recently acquired it. Al-

At Lows Lake

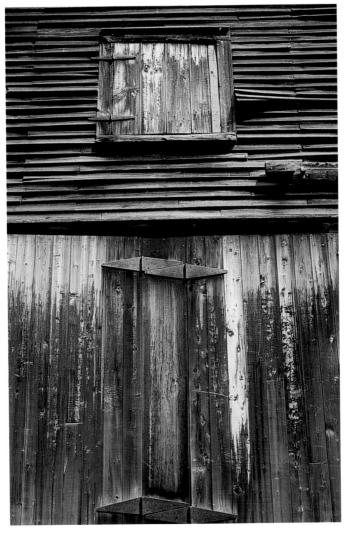

Robin's barn, Keene Valley

though these lands and waters in recent times had been owned by Boy Scout Councils, in an earlier era they had been part of the vast holdings of Abbot Augustus (Gus) Low, who in 1892–96 bought several large tracts, including Bog Lake, Lake Marion, Horseshoe Lake, and Hitchins Pond, totaling about forty-five thousand acres. Low had been in his father's importing and shipping business in New York City and Brooklyn. He was also an inventor of wide repute, and at the time of his death in 1912, only Thomas Edison had more patents registered. Low called his Adirondack enterprises the Horse Shoe Forestry Company. He built a railroad, lumbered much of his land, built a box-making and barrel mill, went into the spring water business (shipped as far away as New York City), developed a sophisticated maple syrup operation (collecting the sap via pipes and troughs), and made wine with grapes shipped in from the finger Lakes. After Low's death his family took over, selling off large tracts of land from time to time, the last being sold to the Suffolk County Boy Scouts in 1973.

Signs identifying shoreline camping sites had been put up by state rangers, but the sites we checked out were not yet cleared, so we chose our own spot on a small island, one that, with a little thrashing around, sported an area just big enough for our small tent and gear. Our cooking area and "dining room" were on a spit of sand that also served as our bathing beach, the water being just barely warm enough for quick dips on this pleasant Memorial Day weekend.

We had a wonderful time exploring bays, adjoining wetlands, and some of the surrounding woods, highlighted by a bushwhack up Grass Pond Mountain, which provides a magnificent overview of this wild and remote neck of the woods. From that first weekend I have been forever grateful that the state had the wisdom and foresight to put these nine thousand acres into the public domain of the Adirondacks. And I have talked to hundreds of others who have had some of their finest Adirondack experiences here. Unfortunately, because of a single private inholding, motorboats and float planes have in recent years substantially interrupted the peace and quiet of the Bog River Flow, above the Upper Dam.

Another lake, actually the largest totally surrounded by state Forest Preserve, which lovers of nonmotorized watercraft will find to their liking, is Lake Lila. Being southwest of Tupper Lake, it can be accessed via state route 30, county routes 10A and 10 (the Sabattis Road), and a rough gravel road that turns left off of the Sabattis Road and dead-ends at a parking area. There is about a one-third mile carry to a fine sand beach and put-in. Lila offers exceptionally attractive campsites, highly scenic paddling, and great swimming. A foot trail from the west end leads to an easy climb to the summit of Frederica (on some maps Smith) Mountain. Although not very high, Frederica offers great views of Lila, and you can even see some of the High Peaks to the northeast.

More wilderness waters are found in the Saint Regis Canoe Area near Saranac Inn. Several different routes coupling ponds with short carries offer excellent paddling, camping, fishing, and swimming, again without the interference of motorboats. The adventurous are encouraged to walk the carry from Long Pond to Mountain Pond and then bushwhack (follow your nose and compass) up Long Pond Mountain, which offers exceptionally rewarding views.

Two Adirondack Wild Rivers that are easily accessed are the Oswegatchie and the Hudson. To paddle the Oswegatchie, put in at Inlet (between Cranberry Lake and Star Lake). Meandering through alder thickets, marshland, and a variety of forest types, the Oswegatchie is a slow-moving, flatwater river that is actually paddled upstream from Inlet. In the 13 miles from Inlet to the foot of High Falls, the drop is barely one foot per mile, so you don't have to be an expert paddler to attempt this trip. Since it is an upstream paddle, medium high to high water in spring or after a heavy rain calls for more experience and the strength of two paddlers. You can continue a ways above High Falls after a carry around the falls, if you are prepared to lift your watercraft

Road past my view

over fallen trees and beaver dams. There are several good camping sites along the way. At about the 11.5-mile point you reach a foot bridge and trail that leads to the Five Ponds and the big trees.

Running the Wild River section of the Hudson is another matter entirely. It is boulder bestrewn, with a very steep gradient, featuring challenging whitewater during medium- to high-water periods. Unless you are an expert whitewater canoeist or kayaker, the way to experience this river is to sign up with one of the several rafting companies that operate out of the Village of Indian Lake. The season starts after ice-out and runs to the latter part of May or so. The put-in point is on the Indian River not very far upstream of its confluence with the Hudson. From here on to North River, you experience a several-hour ride of a lifetime. Most impressive is the section through the Gorge, where you'll encounter the Blue Ledges and Big Nasty Rapids. The outfitters supply you with everything you need, and it's quite safe. An alternative way of seeing at least a part of this wild and scenic stretch of river is to drive out the Northwoods Club Road off route 28N near Minerva. Just before you reach Huntley Pond on your left is a trailhead for the very pleasant two-mile or so hike to the Blue Ledges. Upon reaching the river you can scramble along the boulder-lined north bank (downstream is best) for a ways if the water level is not too high.

Two Scenic Rivers in the State Rivers System are the north fork of the Bouquet and the main branch of the Moose. The north fork is one to experience on foot. It is a very attractive, steep mountain stream with numerous waterfalls and narrow chasms. It features some fine swimming holes. Drive five or six miles south on route 73 from Saint Huberts, and you'll cross a bridge over the north fork. There is a small parking lot on your right just before the bridge, or you can park along the road where it is wide enough. There are well-worn bushwhack trails that start up both sides of the stream. I prefer the trail on the south side. An alternative is to hike the Round Pond trail toward Dix

Mountain. There is a small trailhead parking area for this trail about four miles south of Saint Huberts. You'll pass the very beautiful Round Pond and will need to hike another couple of miles before the trail starts paralleling the north fork.

The main branch of the Moose from McKeever (on route 28 south of Old Forge) to the park boundary is one of the park's most challenging whitewater streams. Only expert boaters should attempt this stretch. But you can see some portions of it by driving along the Moose River Road, which strikes west from McKeever on the south side of the river.

Recreational Rivers in the state system include the west and east branches of the Ausable. Like most Recreational Rivers, they are paralleled by public roads along much of their course. Route 86 between Lake Placid and Wilmington takes you along several miles of the west branch of the Ausable. The great beauty of this often steep-pitched, boulder-laden stream is exceeded by few other park rivers. It is an outstanding fishing stream and includes a "trophy trout" section.

Route 9N between Keene and Jay parallels much of the east branch of the Ausable, as does the Hulls Falls Road, which is a short cutoff road between Keene Valley and Keene. Hulls Falls itself and a fine stretch of the river can be viewed from the Hulls Falls bridge. The Hulls Falls Road is a great running or walking road because of the river views and the quiet, wooded, rural setting.

Another river that must be mentioned is the Raquette, sections of which are Scenic and Recreational and which can be paddled in the Adirondack Park all the way from Blue Mountain Lake to Carry Falls Reservoir. Paul Jamieson calls it "everybody's river. Motorboats churn its waters between the carries except for two sections classified Scenic: the 6 miles from the foot of Long Lake to Raquette Falls, and the 13 miles from Sols Island to Moosehead Rapids. But the attraction of the river far outweighs the noise and congestion. Thousands of canoeists

Black-eyed Susans rioting

Eye on the apple, white-tailed deer

many of the higher mountains regularly. The reporter said, "Some people say most of these Adirondack Mountains and all of the Wilderness Areas might as well have 'keep out' signs on them because only the young and hardy can get into these roadless, nonmotorized accessible places." The senior fellow's chuckle broke into a belly laugh. "I've been climbing these Adirondack Peaks for most of my life, and I'm going to keep climbing them as long as I'm alive and can crawl. The only difference is that I just take a little longer than I used to."

The forty-six High Peaks in the Adirondacks are located in the northeastern quadrant of the park. Lake Placid, Keene, and Keene Valley are villages that are "homes of the High Peaks." And then there are all the other mountains, hundreds of them, scattered over the eastern half of the park, with a few in the southwest; many are as rewarding or more so than several of the High Peaks. The easiest High Peak to climb is Cascade, the trailhead for which is found just uphill of the Cascade Lakes on route 73 on the way from Keene to Lake Placid. This trail gets heavy use, particularly on weekends. So a weekday or winter trip is highly recommended if you want to have a bit of solitude on top. Views of the main range and in all directions are very fine. Equally rewarding ascents, although somewhat more difficult, include hiking Giant from Keene Valley; Algonquin, Wright, or Phelps from Adirondack Loj; and Gothics, Armstrong, and Upper or Lower Wolf Jaws from Johns Brook or the Adirondack Mountain Reserve. Another outstanding mountain jaunt is to do the Brothers and Big Slide from the Garden parking lot out of Keene Valley. Most of the remaining forty-six High Peaks require even more time and effort.

Many of the High Peaks can be approached from two or more alternative routes. Keep in mind that the heaviest use centers around the Adirondack Mountain Club's Adirondack Loj/Heart Lake complex. Choosing alternative approaches, where they exist, is highly recommended. The Garden parking lot in Keene Valley often overflows, making it another good place to avoid if alternative approaches exist

Johns Brook, Keene Valley

bird species. Small mammals such as rabbits have increased in number, attracting coyotes close enough to be observed regularly.

Otter are fairly common in some of the park's lakes and rivers, particularly in areas less accessible to trappers. Fishers and pine martens are uncommon and are always a special "find." The only time I've seen martens is when they have visited high-country campsites, enticed by the irresistible odor of bacon or other redolent attractions. Other characteristic species include snowshoe hare, flying squirrel, and beaver, the latter of which now has a healthy population because of enlightened trapping laws and a restocking program undertaken in the early years of the twentieth century, after beavers had been trapped to extinction. Their dams stand on many a stream today and sometimes flood roads without any permits from the Department of Environmental Conservation!

Black bears are so common that five or six hundred are legally harvested in most years! They are not to be feared, but keep your distance, particularly if you discover them with cubs. The rest of the year they spare little time getting out of your way. As Aldo Leopold wrote in *The Round River:* "The outstanding scientific discovery of the 20th Century is not television, or radio, but rather the complexity of the land organism. Only those who know the most about it can appreciate how little is known about it. The last word in ignorance is the man who says of an animal or plant: 'What good is it?'" . . . To keep every cog and wheel is the first caution of intelligent tinkering."

chapter four

Now you don't see a fish jump anymore. There's no fish to jump and no insects to make them jump. It isn't a matter of trying to lime a lake and stocking fish. The fish have to eat, and they'd just eat one another because there's nothing else. It gets to a certain point where you're going to have to play God again and start all over with the littlest insect.

—BILL MARLOWE
retired forest ranger, Big Moose

Beside the Stilled Waters

When Grace Brown's body, with its yellow skin and half-opened eyes, was pulled out of Big Moose Lake in the Adirondacks in the summer of 1906, the events leading to her death became the subject of Theodore Dreiser's famous novel, *An American Tragedy*. Nine decades later, Big Moose Lake is the scene of a second, far more pervasive American tragedy. This time the victim is the lake itself, an aquatic ecosystem in collapse.

When Chester Gillete rowed his lover, Grace, along the southwest shore of Big Moose, he apparently had murder on his mind. Had he been fishing instead, he might well have caught brook trout, white fish, landlocked salmon, or lake trout. Today, Chester would be out of luck. The acidification of Big Moose has very nearly exterminated these fish. Crayfish, freshwater shrimp, frogs, loons, and otters are rarely seen. All that thrives there now are perch, bullheads, and mud fish. Like hundreds of other Adirondack lakes, Big Moose is the victim of acid rain!

Several years ago, from the top floor of the old main hotel at Covewood Lodge on Big Moose Lake, the young daughters of "Major" and Diane Bowes, the proprietors, called down to their folks: "Please bring us up some good tasting water."

"What kind of nonsense is this?" thought their parents. "They're drinking the same good tap water as we are." A short time later one of the daughters suffered stomach upset and diarrhea. The Bowes had their water tested. The findings showed five times the lead fit for human consumption and revealed copper contamination as well. As it sat in the plumbing, the acidified groundwater, another victim of acid rain, was leaching copper out of the pipes and lead from the solder joints. The copper also caused problems with Covewood's septic system by destroying the necessary anaerobic bacteria.

About that time, state fishery and biology experts had concluded that the demise of fishing in Big Moose was not, as previously believed, the result of tannic acids from beaver activity and forest decay; it was due to acid precipitation.

"The bluest, clearest lakes are the deadest!" What a shocker that was when I heard it back in 1983. I was flying over a heavily waterbodied area in the southwest Adirondacks with acid rain researcher Dr. Carl Schofield of Cornell University and some Scandinavian scientists. After lifting off Seventh Lake near Inlet, we did a loop to the north, over the Pigeon Lake Wilderness, and then headed south over the tens of thousands of acres of the Adirondack League Club. The sulfur-laden air masses, which arrive here from the Midwest (tainted by the emissions from coal-fired power plants, smelters, and other industrial complexes) had not discriminated. They had bathed and killed both publicly owned and privately owned waters through the process of acid deposition. In minutes we had ticked off many casual-

Elk Lake, North Hudson

Lake Lila, late evening

that the most sensitive areas of our nation (the Adirondacks, Appalachians, Rockies, Sierras, San Bernardinos, and the forests from Maine to Georgia) are experiencing increasing acid rain damage.

A bill requiring that emissions of both sulfur dioxide and nitrogen oxide be reduced by 70–75 percent below 1990 levels has been sponsored by New York Senators Charles Schumer and Hillary Clinton and New York Congressmen John Sweeney, Sherwood Boehlert, and John McHugh. It is hoped that, by the time this writing appears in print, this federal legislation will have passed. If not, this writer encourages everyone concerned about the waters and forests of the Adirondack Park and numerous other areas of the United States and Canada to join in advocacy efforts to see this absolute necessity embodied into law. If this essential legislation does pass, follow-up monitoring will be necessary to ensure that the expected reduction in sulfur and nitrogen deposition is actually occurring and that the ponded waters of the Adirondacks are recovering.

In late 1999 I walked along Gill Brook in the Keene Valley area, as

Lake Lila's pines

I have done regularly for more than a quarter of a century. The brook is choked with dead and down trees. Its banks, once lined with sizable red spruce, hemlock, and mixed hardwoods, sports many openings in the forest canopy due to excessive blow-down. I've witnessed this deterioration in many corners of the Adirondack Park. It seems quite possible that the acidification of soils (which, according to soil scientists, releases aluminum, which in turn diminishes root systems) is causing trees to topple over more easily when subjected to strong winds, ice storms, and heavy, wet snowfalls. Forests parkwide appear far less healthy than when I arrived here in 1972. I fear for the future. My friend Major Bowes, mentioned at the beginning of this chapter, has termed acid rain "the AIDS of the forest." I'm afraid he is dead right.

Ozone Depletion and Climate Change

So we've tackled acid rain—maybe. But what about the "ozone hole" and the "greenhouse effect"? It is a sobering thought that, no matter what laws New York passes, no matter that the Forest Preserve is deemed "forever wild" under the state's constitution, we and our cherished landscape are not immune. Scientists have determined that the earth's protective ozone layer is dangerously thinning throughout the year. Political pressure mounts daily to speed up the elimination of chemicals such as chlorofluorocarbons (CFCs), which are used as refrigerants and solvents and which destroy ozone in the upper atmosphere. Other gases that speed up the breakdown of ozone include nitrous oxide (one of acid rain's precursors) and those containing chlorine, fluorine, and bromine.

Measurements of ozone levels above the South Pole in springtime reveal that levels have fallen by 40 percent since 1957. Most of the decrease has occurred since the mid-1970s. The latest studies suggest that ozone levels will fall by a few percentage points during the first half of the twenty-first century—although increases in the ozone-destroying chemicals and gases could cause a more than 10 percent fall in ozone. Changes of just a few percentage points in ozone levels would be enough to let substantially more ultraviolet radiation reach the earth's surface. Because ozone affects the earth's heat balance in several ways, the climate could also be affected by changes in ozone concentrations.

Ultraviolet radiation is responsible for sunburn, snowblindness, eye damage, and skin cancer. It affects plant growth by slowing down photosynthesis and delaying germination in many plants, including trees and crops. Algae are particularly sensitive to ultraviolet radiation, which raises fears that damage to the ozone layer could upset marine ecology and decimate fish populations. As levels of ultraviolet radiation mount, skin cancer—already the most common form of cancer in humans—will become more common. This increase will include even the most lethal form of skin cancer, melanoma. The incidence of eye diseases will increase, and the ability of the body's immune system to cope with infections may well be impaired. In the Adirondacks a great concern could well focus on lowered forest productivity as ultraviolet radiation slows down many aspects of plant growth. In recent years I have traveled to both Australia and New Zealand, where the effects of ozone depletion are the most severe. Skin cancer rates are alarming and rising. Children not wearing hats for protection are sent home from school. Clothing is commonly rated for the degree of sunproofness. Broad-brimmed hats, many with "trailing" neck protection, are popular. There is little doubt that these things will become more commonplace here. Application of sunscreen has for me, and many of my friends, became ritual before going outside for the day.

The greenhouse effect results from the rapidly increasing atmospheric concentration of several gases, particularly carbon dioxide (CO_2). Levels of CO_2, produced primarily when fossil fuels are burned to provide power, are expected to increase by 30 percent during the next fifty years. Current predictions are that the greenhouse effect will

Haystack from Mount Marcy

Lower Cascade Lake, High Peaks Wilderness boundary

ozone returns. Analyses performed by the EPA suggest that even if all ozone-depleting chemicals are phased out it will take a century for conditions in the atmosphere to return even to what they were in 1986.

In late 1997, 150 nations met in Kyoto, Japan, to work toward an agreement to cut greenhouse gas emissions. The pact reached called for developed countries to drastically cut these emissions. In November 1998, delegates from the same nations met in Buenos Aires to set a timetable to carry out the pact. Despite conflicts that clouded the accord, some progress was made—the delegates committed themselves to work on the pact's biggest obstacles over the next few years. Among the obstacles is the United States's position that developing countries, like China and India, need to play a larger role in heading off global warming. To entice developing nations to pursue such a path, America favors a "clean development mechanism," which would give donor nations credit for foreign aid or investments that cut emissions in developing countries. China and India are still resisting calls for the large and populous developing countries to promise emissions cuts.

In early 2001 many nations met again. With the glaring exception

Daisies via fish-eye. Daisies are a prolific exotic
that have adapted rather harmoniously (naturalized)

Whallons Bay, Lake Champlain, Essex

Sugar maple

Snowstorm, Saint Regis Canoe Area

of the United States, they agreed with the principles of the protocol. Without the United States on board, the world cannot possibly meet the targets of the Kyoto Protocol, which calls for industrial countries to cut their greenhouse emissions drastically between 2008 and 2012.

Can this dilemma be solved? The answer depends, to some extent, on the Bush administration and its future position on this issue. It also depends on whether the United States is successful in obtaining commitments from the developing world and putting in place a complex scheme for trading emissions permits and credits.

Other Pollution Concerns

Other pollution concerns in the Adirondacks involve solid waste, freshwater pollution, and pesticides. The soul-searching that has gone on in the Adirondack Park over what to do about solid waste echoes the concerns of people in the rest of New York State and the United States: What is the most environmentally sound way to get rid of that which cannot be reused and recycled? How can we afford new approaches to solid waste disposal and the closure of nonconforming, polluting landfills? How can we find markets for such recycled materials as glass, metal, and plastics?

State-of-the-art, lined landfills and burn plants have been explored. Either option has its share of problems. Studies indicate that manmade liners ultimately leak—it's only a matter of when. The best bet seems to locate landfills where there is a good depth of naturally occurring clay, away from wetlands, waterways, and aquifers.

The concern over burn plants has to do with air pollution and how to dispose of the resulting ash, which is often determined to be a hazardous waste if toxics and heavy metals are not removed before burning. Apparently, air pollution concerns can to some extent be minimized if the burning process is carefully operated and monitored, including the maintenance of high enough temperatures to obtain more

Rainbow Falls, Saint Huberts

complete combustion. Yet there remains the problem of heavy metals in the smoke.

Pollution of the park's freshwater (lakes, ponds, rivers, streams) results from both point and nonpoint sources (or runoff). Upgrading existing industrial, municipal, and individual sewage treatment facilities and systems helps a lot, as does adequate setback, siting, and operational and maintenance requirements of individual septic systems and industrial and municipal facilities. As more development occurs in a watershed, however, nonpoint pollution, or runoff, can outstrip the gains made in proper handling of point source pollution. This occurs because development removes naturally occurring vegetation and replaces it with structures, pavement, and other less porous surfaces. This leads to increased quantities of pesticides, fertilizers, oil and fuels from motor vehicles, and other man-made polluting substances entering running and ponded waters as runoff.

One of the best ways to improve degraded freshwater systems and

Whallons Bay, Lake Champlain, Essex

On Pitchoff Mountain, Sentinel Wilderness

to maintain those that are still of high quality is to limit development, require that it be set back farther from stream banks and shorelines, and restrict the amount of vegetation that is cleared. A Wild, Scenic, and Recreational Lakes System, modeled after the Wild, Scenic, and Recreational Rivers System, which would strive to preserve lake shorelines in varying degrees of their natural state, could be most helpful in both restoring and preserving the water quality of the park's lakes and ponds.

Chemical pesticides have been widely used in the Adirondack Park to control blackflies and mosquitoes, to remove unwanted vegetation in power line and highway rights of way, and to keep golf courses weed- and fungus-free. Fortunately, a relatively nonpolluting, very narrow spectrum (kills mainly target insects) biological control called bti has proven to be a healthy, more effective alternative to chemical control of blackflies and mosquitoes.

Public awareness and pressure have also mounted to eliminate the use of chemical herbicides on rights of way near power lines and highways. The chemicals that have been used are highly suspect from a wildlife and human health standpoint, and studies have shown that manual control (cutting) can be achieved for the same or lower cost. Studies have shown, as well, that the use of chemical pesticides can be substantially reduced or substituted for without affecting the quality of the turf on golf courses. The Adirondack Park Agency has developed an effective means of evaluating the risk factors associated with golf-course pesticides and has in its project review process declined to approve the use of a wide variety of such pesticides. This, unfortunately, relates only to golf courses that are proposed to be built. Legislation is needed to require critical review of the chemical pesticiding programs of existing golf courses.

More and more people are concluding that the Adirondack Park should be as free of chemical pesticides as possible. Only those pesticides that have been proven to be relatively harmless to humans and

Barney and Mark, Wadhams

natural systems should be allowed. The park could lead the way to reversing the present national policy, as presided over by the federal Environmental Protection Agency, on pesticide use, which in reality has been to allow the use of chemical pesticides until they have been proven guilty. There has been some reform of the EPA pesticide review and registration process in recent years to now require full and adequate testing of all of the several hundred active ingredients used in chemical pesticides. In the interim, while this time-consuming testing is undertaken, many highly suspect chemicals continue to invade our air, water, and food to the detriment of humans and wildlife.

chapter five

We've been fortunate to have a state agency like the Adirondack Park Agency that stands up for its purpose to preserve the Park. It's far too easy to succumb to business' seduction and put less restraint on development, but the issue of jobs is political, not ecological. That short-term concern, however, mustn't cloud the long-range vision of park preservationists. They must concentrate not on the next four years, not on the next 25, but on the next century ... The Park has been here for New Yorkers for 100 years and must remain.

—GREG NORTON, *Elizabethtown Valley News*

Will the Forest Be Unbroken?

Two days before the end of 1990, a few friends and I headed out into a soggy, 55°F day, in a steady rain, for a walk. Much to our chagrin the snow was mostly gone. We had wished to go on a cross-country ski outing into the back country somewhere, but we settled for a hike over Big and Little Crow near Keene. Despite the foggy conditions when we left our car on East Hill, I was surprised to find that we had views from the summits of these two small mountains. The forested tops of some lower hills stuck out of the fog-shrouded valley below, while broken, higher clouds whizzed by. Subtle contrasts of various shades of blacks and grays and the movement rendered the scene like some beckoning Shangri-la. It was a breathtaking, unexpected reward. I thought, "Most people would think we're nuts to be out on such a miserable day. But they are missing something very special." As on similar days when

I had hesitantly headed off into the mountains, I learned once again that the Adirondacks' rare beauty cannot be masked even on the worst of days. During the short hike between the two Crow summits, the paper birch forest seemed to generate its own magic light. Mist, shimmering off shallow pools that the steady rains had created, added additional wonder.

The intimacy and beauty of these Adirondack forests and mountains have captured the fancy of countless men and women. That is why, no doubt, people get involved in such heated debate over what should and shouldn't be done to maintain the unique character of this place. The emergence of the Adirondack Park Agency (APA) and its regulatory powers over private lands in the early 1970s started a near-revolution that lingers today.

In May 1973, the Adirondack Park Agency–authored Adirondack Park Land Use and Development Plan went into effect; this plan dictates how private land is to be used and developed. Before 1973, most of the debate and controversy in the Adirondacks had been focused on the state-owned, Forest Preserve portion of the Adirondack Park. For almost a century some people had been interminably bothered by a forest that existed solely for spiritual, recreational, and ecological purposes. Cutting the state forests, these detractors had argued, would bring cash to the state treasury, and opening up the woods would increase the number of deer, since shrubs and other "early successional" plants are what deer prefer to eat.

The preservationist, protectionist sentiment had prevailed, however, and the publicly owned Forest Preserve to this day remains "forever wild." But as of 1973 the use of all of the park's private lands was to be guided by state-imposed land-use controls. All private lands in the park had been subjected to natural resource–based studies and mapping. Except in the park's hamlets, the largest of which has a population of six thousand people, limitations on building densities were now in place. These densities took into account such factors as soils,

Looking over the unbroken forest from Rooster Comb Mountain

Mixed woods from Rooster Comb Mountain

slope, elevation; wildlife and plant communities; wild, scenic, and recreational rivers; scenic and open space resources; and surface and groundwater characteristics. Growth and development would be directed to where it would least impair valuable natural resources. Development projects that had the potential to cause effects beyond their immediate areas would be subject to APA review and permitting. New development on lakes, ponds, and rivers would also be subject to shoreline restrictions, including minimum lot width and minimum setbacks for structures and septic systems, and there would be limitations on the clearing of vegetation.

Because the park is rugged country and biologically rich, on about 50 percent of the private land the building density is limited to fifteen single-family dwellings per square mile to ensure that the landscape can handle the development and that wildlife habitat is not sacrificed. That averages out to just under 43 acres per dwelling, but clustering is encouraged. Smaller lots can be subdivided and built upon as long as the 43-acre average per individual ownership is not exceeded. More developable and less fragile private lands are zoned more leniently, with 8.5, 3.2, and 1.5 acres on the average being required per dwelling. Map amendments can be applied for and are approved if applicants can make a convincing case that their land has been incorrectly mapped and classified. Preexisting lots of record, held before the implementation of the law in May 1973, can be built upon no matter what the size, as long as foundations and septic systems can be accommodated. Land owned before May 1973 can also be subdivided into substandard lots among immediate family.

Problems

Opposition to these rules and regulations began to build from day 1. This is not surprising, since 90 percent of the park's villages and towns had previously imposed no zoning or land-use regulations of any kind.

Seasons competing above Keene Valley

Clear Pond, North Hudson

Landowners were being required to take a giant step. Many Realtors and developers and those who make a living in the building trades saw these restrictions as punitive. Joined by landowners who had counted on being able to subdivide and sell lots to supplement their income or get them through their retirement years, those wanting to develop the Adirondacks began to capture the attention of the media and politicians, at both state and local levels. Adirondackers in the state legislature attempted to weaken the law and later to abolish the APA. Lawsuits were initiated, charging that taking land without compensation was unlawful and that the state was usurping the planning and zoning functions generally conveyed to local governments. Protestors swarmed the state capitol and state legislature. Debate was intense, but opposition efforts were to no avail. APA law remained intact. In the opinion of the courts and the majority of New York's citizenry, there is an overriding state interest in preserving the area as a wild, open space park.

In the late 1980s, pressures to subdivide the park's rural back country intensified. The number of development projects increased dramatically, as well, placing increased pressures on the park's vulnerable shorelines, roadsides, and privately owned open space. In the twenty-year period between 1967 and 1987, twenty-one thousand single-family homes and sixty-five hundred building lots had been added to the park. Sales of subdivided property tripled between 1982 and 1985; by 1988 they had doubled again. Loopholes in the APA law, in particular the provision allowing denser development along shorelines, became more obvious as formerly pristine places like the southern basin of Lake George experienced problems with water quality.

Environmentalists led by the Adirondack Council and the media called upon the governor to act. John Oakes wrote an "Adirondack S.O.S." in the *New York Times:*

He [Governor Cuomo] could work for strengthening the Adirondack Park Agency Act, which has loopholes wide enough to drive a bulldozer through and several have already been driven. He could support revision of the Park's zoning plan, which potentially permits another half million homes in the Park. He could push the Legislature to enact a land transfer tax—similar to the ones now successfully working in Martha's Vineyard and Nantucket—to provide a continuously renewable financial base for environmentally significant purchases . . . The Adirondack land rush is a good place to show his environmental teeth, if any.

In a matter of days, the governor took up the challenge and responded:

A few weeks ago I decided to establish a Commission on the Adirondacks in the 21st Century, to examine the Adirondacks in a comprehensive way, to suggest what needs to be done to preserve this magnificent legacy. More than 100 years ago, a group of New Yorkers wrote into law the simple truth that we could no longer hope to survive if we went on destroying the natural surroundings that support us all. They taught us that we must learn to think of ourselves as more than creatures of a single moment. While much has changed, one immutable fact remains unchanged. Despite our technological proficiency, we are still dependent on an ecosystem that is fragile and interconnected.

Cuomo's charge to the commission, to recommend steps essential to preserve the Adirondack Park's great reaches of open space, working landscapes, and intact rural communities, was addressed with dispatch, since the commission had little more than a year to deliver. The commission fully recognized the potential of New York State to set an example of wise and lasting stewardship over both private and public lands in the Adirondack Park, an example for how people can harmoniously live alongside wilderness. As the commission termed it, "There is room in this Park for people and nature to live together in mutual sustainable development, where the call of the loon and the buzz of the logger's saw can coexist."

The Commission on the Adirondacks in the Twenty-first Century, after a series of hearings attended by more than four thousand people and after their year of intense study, issued its recommendations in May 1990. The results were immediate and dramatic. People threatened to burn the woods, burn the homes of preservationists, and take up arms. I was told that I had a bounty on my head. A caller told my answering machine that the Adirondack Council's offices would be burned if the proposed Gleneagles Development (a combination of hotel restoration, more than three hundred condominiums and townhouse units, and subdivision of a highly scenic area into a hundred-plus lots) was not approved by the Adirondack Park Agency. I was singled out, no doubt, as the executive director of the Adirondack Council at the time. The council opposed the project as initially proposed for being inappropriately large and incompatible with the park's natural and rural character.

One Monday morning council staff found swastikas on the office windows. An eviction proclamation was affixed to the door, signed by several local citizens. A mock tombstone had been shoved into a barrel of potting soil. On the previous Saturday, about ten men, most or all of

Keene Valley forest readying for winter

Afternoon light flatters the High Peaks Wilderness

Late evening, Beaver Meadow, Adirondack Mountain Reserve, Saint Huberts

whom had just left a rally protesting the recommendations of the Commission on the Adirondacks in the Twenty-first Century, had pulled up in front of Adirondack Council staffer Eric Siy's house in several pickup trucks and a couple of cars. Storming onto Siy's porch they had pounded on the door. Eric opened his door to receive them and later remarked that he had felt "like a lynch mob had come to get me." The first words out of their spokesman were "we'll see you buried." Siy was then told that he'd better start packing because "all Adirondack Council staffers are going to be moving out of the Adirondack Park." Another remarked that "people are ready to start shooting." As fortune would have it, Siy's next-door neighbor, a county sheriff, intervened, and the belligerent crew had been forced to leave.

As the summer of 1990 wore on, things became more violent. "Many fed-up Adirondack natives" sent an anonymous letter to the council:

There will be no more—better read that again, NO MORE, talks, negotiation, or meetings of any kind with your group of arrogant, garbage wrapped in gift paper bastards. You have all forfeited your constitutional rights here in the Adirondacks. We natives have lived on bear and venison meat, gone without the basic necessities of life, and shed our blood for this area, and by God, you and yours will never live long enough to enjoy it. You had better be ready to take it with blood . . . have you considered the ultimate??? The whole damned park of yours burning in hundreds of places at once. If we can't have our land, without interference from you idiots, then no one will have it!!!

What could a commission recommend that would, like a blast furnace, fuel such a heated, emotional, life-threatening controversy? First off, many folks formed the mistaken impression that the state would take their land by eminent domain to expand and round out the state-owned Forest Preserve. The Commission Report contained a map identifying high-priority, privately owned lands that the state should

Bluets in pleasing overpopulation

acquire, *but only* as they are offered up on the market by willing sellers. The false impression that the state would take land through condemnation was at the heart of the opponents' fear, anger, and hostility. A complex land condemnation case, not explained by the state because of pending litigation, gave rise to the impression on the part of some that their land would be next. This just wasn't true. The state had moved to take land by eminent domain in the Adirondacks only a couple of times during the last quarter of a century. The state uses the power rarely and selectively when it feels that the public good will be served.

Several charismatic individuals started organizations specifically to oppose the report. Within five years, all of them would see their influence and membership disappear. But the ones who used terrorist tactics made life uncomfortable for environmentalists. One of the main reasons that the property-rights groups were able to seize attention was the complexity of the report itself. The report listed 245 unprioritized recommendations. There was an assumption that all would be pursued with equal vigor. Adirondack locals assumed that the environmental community had the influence to persuade Governor Cuomo and the legislature to enact the entire document without debate.

Misinformation and lack of information regarding the commission's recommendations didn't help matters. Since the commission, unfortunately, went out of business even before their report was made public, interpretation of the report was sorely lacking. Commission Executive Director George Davis exhausted himself in a series of solo explanation sessions around the state. But when Davis appeared before some Adirondack-area audiences, he was booed by a hostile crowd of people who had already made up their minds that they didn't want to be confused by facts and that the whole report should be discarded. Quite expectedly, Realtors and developers working behind the scenes, preying upon the emotions of landowners, worked them into a frenzy of opposition.

The Commission Report included some very tough recommendations that went light years beyond existing law. On about 85 percent of the park's private land, where presently 43 or 8.5 acres are required on the average for new lots and housing units, most future development would be prohibited. But the development rights could be sold to owners of lands in less restrictive areas or to the state. This did little, however, to satisfy owners who planned to split off some of their land for their children or other family members. And the $100 per acre figure that the commission recommended the state pay for development rights was vehemently deplored by some. Commission members later admitted this was way out of line and that the price should be based upon fair market value.

The commission recommended tough remediation measures to restore the scenic quality of shorelines and roadsides. They also recommended that commercial ventures, other than those related to agriculture and forestry, be primarily restricted to hamlets and their immediate environs. The commission's suggested limit of five individuals per group intending to camp on Forest Preserve land found much disfavor.

The vast majority of the commission's recommendations were fair and insightful and would, if imposed, be beneficial to all parties. The lot of park residents would benefit economically, socially, and ecologically. It is unfortunate that a few recommendations that were thought by some to be extreme caused the Commission Report to be shelved in its entirety. But it is comforting that proposed legislation offered by both the governor's office and the legislature in early 1992 resurrected several of the commission's recommendations.

Many local residents take issue with the process, which they perceive to have repeatedly cut local citizens and local government officials out of the decision-making function. On this matter there are broadly divergent opinions. Since the inception of the Park Agency, there has been a provision in the law to encourage a partnership between local and state governments. Towns developing Adirondack Park Agency (APA)–approved local land-use plans (which must include zoning restrictions, subdivision regulations, and a sanitary code that deals with sewage treatment) regain some of the project review and permitting powers that were conveyed to the APA by the state leg-

Top of Saddleback in the Jay Wilderness

Mountain Pond near Paul Smiths

Young maple forest, Keese Mill

islature in 1973. This program has met with limited success. Local planning monies provided by the state have been intermittent, and many towns don't have the resources or political will to move forward. Some just don't understand the law. Local officials still state publicly that they should throw out their APA-approved local plan and get the APA off their backs.

Membership on the APA (the makeup of the decision-making body of commissioners) is also controversial. How many members should there be, who should appoint them, how long should they serve, who or what should they represent?

Solutions

These matters have been debated since the APA was established, and they no doubt will continue to be heated topics into the foreseeable future. Local government must play a greater role in land-use planning and control functions in the park, at least where private lands are concerned. The state-owned lands of the Adirondack Park, however, are as much of a concern of all the people of the state as the federally owned public lands in Alaska and other states are to all Americans. In other words, if the majority of the people in New York State want a road into a state-owned Wilderness Area closed to motor vehicles, it

Maple leaves at Gill Brook

shall be so, regardless of whether a group of local citizens feel that this is unjust.

For local government to become more involved in the regulation of private lands in the Adirondack Park, some things need to happen. The state must provide more and consistent financial and technical assistance to local governments. Local government officials need to broaden their views beyond their own political jurisdiction (some have done so) and be willing to help formulate and support local land-use plans that truly balance environmental and park protection with community and economic development. The APA should offer training sessions for local officials who have little or no prior exposure to land-use issues. Counties should be enabled to develop land-use/zoning plans for towns and villages and should be required to do so if municipalities fail to act within a reasonable period. And finally, state government, supported by the environmental community, must give local officials and local people more of an opportunity to present their ideas and sentiments regarding private land-use issues. How to achieve the latter requires hard, creative thought. Meeting this need is of extreme importance, however, since it is all too obvious that the legitimate interest of these parties deserves a hearing and can contribute a dimension of thought that has heretofore been little heard. An ombudsman

Lake Colby, Saranac Lake Village

working out of the Park Agency offices could investigate citizen complaints and assist in achieving fair determinations for those seeking permits from the APA.

We need to find the means now to ensure that present and future subdivision and development be done on a scale that will preserve this special place in some semblance of what exists today. We must pay more homage to this Adirondack land if we are to keep intact this forever-wild state forest, this natural open-space park for which New Yorkers have fought so hard during the past century. We must see this land, these woods, as common ground, a gift to all New Yorkers and Americans now living and yet to come. This is not to suggest that landowners here should be forced to open up their lands and houses and invite everyone in. What it does suggest is that the park should be considered holistically, emphasizing the importance of the whole and the interdependence of its parts. Dissection, or subdivision of the land into smaller and smaller pieces; overdevelopment; transformation of primary forest and agricultural lands; pollution by sewage, pesticides, solid waste, excess noise or light; desecration of scenic and open space resources—these are practices that threaten the park's organic wholeness. Keeping a parcel of land intact; allowing only low-density, well-designed, and well-sited development; preserving critical farm and forest land; and keeping the land pollution-free are practices reflecting stewardship, and these actions deserve to be encouraged through recognition and reward.

Some of the large, private clubs of the Adirondacks have been exemplary stewards. From the top of Gothics Mountain, it is impossible to differentiate between the Ausable Club's Adirondack Mountain Reserve's lands and the higher-elevation Forest Preserve lands. Only canoes and guide boats ply the waters of the club's Upper and Lower Ausable Lakes. The dozen or so camps on the upper lake (there are no camps on the lower lake) are set back from the shoreline and painted dark, earthen colors, and little vegetation has been cut. You'd never know they were there. The Ausable Club has been implementing many of the commission's most controversial recommendations for well over a century. Several other large private clubs have preserved large tracts of Adirondack land. They deserve to be applauded for their care and efforts. Though few have opened their lands to the public as the Ausable Club has, they have nevertheless kept tens of thousands of acres in an undeveloped state, contributing to clean air and pure waters and preserving views and critical open space. They include the Adirondack League Club, Northwoods Club, Tahawus Club, Wilmurt Lake Club, and Underwood Club, among others.

Several private individuals, some owning tens of thousands of acres, have for decades maintained private, undeveloped "parks." Some outstanding examples of land stewardship in America are hidden back in these hills and mountains. Fortunately, the majority of all Adirondack landowners have taken good care of their land. The challenge is to keep it this way and to encourage stewardship in all quarters. Stewardship is key to the park's future. I am not talking about the stewardship of the shallow resource management mentality of the man-over-nature sort. Instead, I am talking about humans seeing themselves as "plain members" of the biotic community, in which they break through their anthropocentric illusions and, in Aldo Leopold's words, "think like a mountain." In doing so they discover the broader and deeper community of trees, rivers, mountains, and animals.

I own a seventy-acre farm, including a hundred-year-old house, a couple of barns, and an old granary. The person who sold it to me conditioned the deed so that no additional dwellings can be built on the parcel. I can build accessory structures like a garage or chicken coop, but not any type of unit that includes water or septic systems that could house another individual or family. I didn't resist this condition of sale. The seventy acres are mostly good farmland, presently in hay and alfalfa. I lease this portion to a neighboring farmer. Building another dwelling unit anywhere on my land would either squander pro-

East Hill, Keene

ductive farmland, be unsightly, or both, since the seventy acres are open fields that are highly visible and contribute to the extraordinary beauty of the Champlain Valley. I am aware that taxes and upkeep costs may increase to the point where, particularly after retirement, I may encounter financial difficulties. Yet I am glad that I do not have the option to subdivide or develop any of my land because it should be retained intact as a small, productive farm. I am its steward now. After I move away, pass away, or am pressured into selling, that stewardship will pass on to someone or some others willing to own a parcel that cannot be subdivided. My stewardship of this land to some extent results from outside forces. My land is classified Resource Management under the APA Act, which would probably allow me to sell off a lot or two. My former landlady, the person from whom I bought the farm, has further restricted its use. But much of my stewardship is self-imposed. I don't want to see the land use change. I do not dump any kind of waste on the land. I use only naturally occurring, organic insecticides in my garden.

My motivation for all of this lies in looking at land ownership as a

Maple revelry

responsibility and an opportunity to practice a lifestyle that must become more commonly accepted and desired if we are to survive on this overpopulated, polluted planet. But first I had to recognize that I could *afford* to be a good land steward. I have a decent income and do not have any significant financial obligations beyond a mortgage and the other normal expenses that include utilities, food, clothing, and transportation. But others are not so fortunate, and we need to encourage stewardship by incentives, such as tax relief, the acquisition of development rights (or conservation easements) for fair market value payment, or other payments or subsidies.

Those who preceded us in claiming portions of the Adirondacks, both the Algonquin and the Iroquois, had an innate sense of stewardship. They saw land as a mother who nurtured and provided for them and other living creatures as their brothers and sisters. Additionally, these native Americans were few in number, established few permanent settlements, and used the Adirondacks primarily as a hunting and fishing ground. Alteration of the land community was slight. This is not to say that the Indians of the northeastern forests did not cause ecological change. In some areas they used fires or girdled trees to make clearings in the forest. They harvested fish and wildlife for food and clothing and to use as barter. The changes to the landscape were temporary and slight, however. The Iroquois took a long-term view of things, guided by the concept of the seventh generation, which held that "in our every deliberation we must consider the effect of our decisions on the next seven generations."

The Algonquins saw themselves as part of nature, at peace with the land, lakes and rivers, animals, fish, and birds. Through their close relationship with their natural environment, they developed a philosophy based on respect for all living things. Respect for everything and everyone on mother earth led to their ideal brotherhood.

It was Aldo Leopold, writing in his *Sand County Almanac* (1949), who saw the wisdom of relating to the natural environment in the "Indian way" as a matter of good scientific sense. He called conservation a state of harmony between humans and the land. "Land," said Leopold, "is not merely soil; it is a fountain of energy flowing through a circuit of soils, plants and animals." The study of the interrelations of living things and their environment is the science called *ecology*. Acquaintance with ecology makes us aware that our natural environment, the land, is a community to which we belong. This "ecological conscience" teaches us that our true place as humans is as a dependent member of a biotic community. From this understanding springs a sense that a thing is right when, in Leopold's words, "it tends to preserve the integrity, stability, and beauty of the biotic community. It is wrong when it tends otherwise." Trying to do right with the land is the basis of stewardship and the land ethic.

The acquisition by the state of some key tracts of private land or the acquisition of development and other land rights on these properties is essential to the Adirondack Park's long-term protection. Several very attractive properties that are or may be on the market in the future have enormous recreation potential or ecological significance, or both. They include such gems as Follensby Pond, southeast of Tupper Lake; the remaining lands of the coveted Whitney estate, with its extensive system of lakes, ponds, and streams; Preston Ponds adjoining the High Peaks Wilderness on the south; some of the lands of the Finch-Pruyn Paper Company, including OK Slip Falls, the Hudson River Gorge, and Boreas Ponds; and portions of International Paper's vast holdings.

These large-acreage, wild, open space tracts will have two likely buyers—speculators/developers or the State of New York. Purchase by the former will probably lead to subdivision, loss of present character, and posted signs. Purchase by the latter will keep the lands intact and pristine, and all of us will be invited in. Which makes more sense? Which is better for the park, its flora and fauna, and the people?

In the thirty years since I've been in the park, the state has acquired outstanding lands and interests in land, including ownership of the

Adirondack guide boat, the region's unique watercraft

Santanoni Preserve near Newcomb, land and easements surrounding Lake Lila, a combination of land and access easements at the Ausable Club's Adirondack Mountain Reserve at Saint Huberts, land and access at Lows Lake near Sabattis, three miles of Lake Champlain shoreline, 15,000 acres of the Whitney estate including all of Little Tupper Lake and nine other lakes and ponds, and, most recently, fee title acquisition of 29,000 acres of river corridors and conservation easements over 100,000 acres of lands belonging to Champion International Paper Company. These properties offer recreational opportunities and scenic quality rivaling anything of their kind on this planet. And they are available to anyone wishing to go there for fishing, hunting, hiking, gawking, and a host of other recreational pursuits. Yet some people irrationally decry the state acquiring any such additional properties and land interests.

That the Adirondack Park has national significance was brought to light yet once again when, in the late 1980s and early 1990s, its forests

Skiing into the blizzard, Lost Lake

Woodsmen spare this tree

Protecting the earth, protecting national parks and federal wilderness areas, protecting the Adirondack Park, and protecting those little chunks of wild land that can still be found in our backyards are dependent upon people. The determination to defend these areas and prevent their conversion and loss can be assured through the development of our perceptive faculty. Within the Adirondack woods and other wild places is a never-ending opportunity for expanding perception. All we need to do is train ourselves to see clearly and understand our natural surroundings. With perception of natural processes can come a vision of what Aldo Leopold called "the incredible intricacies of the plant and animal (and human) community—the intrinsic beauty of the organism called America."

We and our political leaders, with the governor at the head, need to forever preserve those very critical elements of this live-in park that are now so vulnerable. The working forests and farms must be kept intact to the greatest degree possible. The roadsides and waterways need to be kept uncluttered because they are the "windows" through which all of us most frequently experience the mountains, forests, waters, and fields that make the park what it is. Finding a way to keep large, privately owned back country land parcels intact is the greatest challenge to ensuring the park's future because these unbroken forests make the park what it is.

Significant progress in achieving lasting protection of the Adirondack Park has happily occurred since Governor George Pataki's administration took over in the mid-1990s. This seems mostly due to his responsiveness and that of his staff. They want to do the right thing for the Adirondack Park and are willing to work with groups like the Adirondack Council for the betterment of the park's wildlands, working landscapes, and human communities.

In July 1996 the Adirondack Council named Governor Pataki Conservationist of the Year, noting that the governor had done more during the preceding twelve months to help the park's environment than had any other person. Pataki surprised the entire state when he proposed a $1.75 billion Clean Water/Clean Air Bond Act, which subsequently was enacted into law. Both the environment and the economy of the Adirondack Park have been strengthened by increasing open space protection, reducing pollution, and relieving tax burdens on local residents. Highlights of open space protection have included the acquisition of 15,000 acres of the Whitney estate, including the largest privately owned lake in the Northeast, and more recently the protection of approximately 140,000 acres of Champion International Paper Company lands. Seventy miles of river closed to the public for a century have been reopened for public use. More than 110,000 acres of productive forest land will be spared from development pressures and fragmentation. For the Adirondack Park this constitutes the largest land conservation and protection deal of all time.

Governor Pataki has been tough on acid rain, initiating legal action against the federal Environmental Protection Agency (EPA) for granting pollution regulation waivers to states upwind of the Adirondacks, whose smokestacks and automobiles are causing acid rain and smog in New York. Pataki's State Health Department has helped to educate the public to the dangers of acid rain as it relates to mercury contamination. Some of the mercury is coming into the area from the same smoke that causes acid rain. The remainder is being leached out of the

Sunset from Haystack Mountain, High Peaks Wilderness

soil and rock when acid rain depletes a watershed's buffering capacity (the naturally occurring alkalinity that can neutralize acidification).

More recently, Governor Pataki has joined forces with the governors of seven northeastern states to again sue the EPA in an effort to force that agency to enact new pollution controls for nitrogen oxides in the Midwest. Additionally, he has been a strong advocate, calling on Congress to enact legislation that will finally reduce acid rain to the point of dead lakes beginning to recover. In the spring of 2000, Pataki signed into law legislation prohibiting New York utilities, which are now cleaner than required by federal law, from selling their unused pollution allowances to out-of-state plants that pollute New York with sulfur dioxide–laden emissions.

More challenges face this progressive Pataki administration. Thousands more acres of commercial forest land are either on the market or likely to be or are crying out for a conservation easement acquisition to enable their owners to achieve a reasonable profit margin. This is equally true for thousands of acres of Champlain Valley farmland, where purchase of easements and the state's sharing of real property taxes could revitalize and save family farms. Acid rain legislation must get through Congress. The New York State Department of Environmental Conservation needs to be more effective and careful in their administration of the Adirondack Park's publicly owned Forest Preserve; additional staffing is necessary. And surely, the Adirondack Park Agency could benefit, as could its clientele, from additional staffing to stay abreast of its enormous workload. Indications are that Pataki and crew can and will meet this and other, yet unforeseen, challenges. They need our encouragement.

It is now or never for the Adirondacks if we are to preserve forever that which is its most priceless and rarest quality—wildness. It is time to hold onto as much of it as we can for, as Thoreau said, "In wildness is the preservation of the world." We are well into the second century of the Adirondack Park. What better time to act than now to make this the true park it has the potential to be, to ensure that the Adirondacks will forever be a wild island of hope for New Yorkers and the world, and to serve as a global model for integrated land use and conservation. The second hundred years promise to be no easier than the first. But if we set our sights high enough, we can succeed. As in the past, what's needed are a few people of vision and determination who can lead and a populace that recognizes the wisdom in keeping the great Adirondack forest unbroken. According to Paul Schaefer, a long-term Adirondack conservationist: "The great natural resources that comprise the forest preserve and the park as we know it today remain because there was vision a century ago and there were statesmen who made the vision a reality. At no time in Adirondack history have there been more opportunities to enhance the park than exist now. Let us be up and doing!"

LOCATION:

In the northernmost portion of New York State, the Adirondack Park is roughly bounded on the north by the Saint Lawrence River and on the south, generally, by the Mohawk Valley. It extends westward nearly to Lake Ontario, with Lake Champlain and Lake George as the eastern boundary.

SIZE:

The park comprises 6 million acres (9,375 square miles), which is one-fifth of the entire area of New York State, about the size of Vermont, and nearly three times the area of Yellowstone National Park.

OWNERSHIP:

Of the total 6 million acres, 2.8 million acres (47%) are state-owned, constitutionally protected Adirondack Forest Preserve belonging to all the people of New York State, and 3.2 million acres (53%) are private lands devoted principally to forestry, agriculture, and open-space recreation. These public and private lands intermingle in a complex, "crazy-quilt" pattern.

POPULATION:

There are 130,000 permanent and 130,000 seasonal residents.

ECONOMY:

Industries include tourism, forest products, agriculture, mining, and public service (government).

GEOGRAPHY:

The western and southern Adirondacks are a gentle landscape of hills, lakes, ponds, and streams. In the northeast are the High Peaks, more than forty mountains over 4,000 feet (including ten alpine summits) spread over twelve hundred square miles. The highest is Mount Marcy at 5,344 feet. These mountains are survivors of the most ancient geographic formation in North America; the erosion-resistant bedrock, accounting for the height of the mountains, is an estimated 1.2 billion years old. The eastern slopes of these mountains descend to the fertile valley of Lake Champlain. Much of the lake is within the Adirondack Park.

FLORA AND FAUNA:

A variety of life zones results in a diversity of plants and animals: open marsh and lakeshore, spruce swamp and bog, northern hardwood forest, mixed forest, upper spruce slope, subalpine, and alpine. The spruce/fir and beech/birch/maple associations reach their crowning glory in Adirondack forests. The fisher, pine marten, bald eagle, and spruce grouse are distinctive wildlife. Thirty tree species are native to the park. Wildflowers abound, and hundreds of species of shrubs, herbs, and grasses may be encountered in a single day's outing. Animal life includes 50 species of mammals, 297 species of birds (193 nesting), 30 species of reptiles and amphibians, and 66 species of fish.

The Adirondacks form the headwaters for most or part of five major basins: Lake Champlain and the Hudson, Black, Saint Lawrence, and Mohawk Rivers. Within the park are 2,800 lakes and ponds and 1,500 miles of rivers fed by more than 30,000 miles of brooks and streams.

RECREATION:

The range of year-round outdoor recreational opportunities is unparalleled in the eastern United States. The Adirondack Park offers boating of all kinds, horseback riding, camping, picnicking, hiking, mountaineering, hunting, fishing, swimming, waterskiing, downhill and cross-country skiing, ice skating, ice boating, snowmobiling, and snowshoeing. There are two thousand miles of foot trails throughout the park, more than half of them state-maintained. A north-south wilderness trail runs 130 miles from Lake Placid to Northville. A popular canoe route begins at Old Forge in the southwest and follows a string of lakes, ponds, rivers, and portages nearly one hundred miles to Tupper Lake and the Saranac Lakes in the north-central region.

resource organizations

Adirondack Council (park advocacy), P.O. Box D-2, Elizabethtown,
New York 12932; (518)873-2240; www.adirondackcouncil.org

Adirondack Mountain Club (recreation, advocacy), Lake George,
New York 12845; (518)668-4447; www.adk.org

Adirondack Museum (heritage interpretation), Blue Mountain Lake,
New York 12812; (518)352-7311; www.adirondackmuseum.org

Adirondack Nature Conservancy/Adirondack Land Trust (land protection), Keene Valley, New York 12943; (518)576-2082;
www.nature.org

Adirondack North Country Association (Adirondack economy),
Saranac Lake, New York 12983; (518)891-6200;
www.adirondack.org

Adirondack Park Agency (private land regulation, park planning),
Ray Brook, New York 12977; (518)891-4050;
www.northnet.org/adirondackparkagency

Adirondack Park Visitor Interpretive Centers (providing park information and interpreting the park through exhibits, audio-visual presentations, and nature trails): Paul Smiths, New York 12970; (518)327-3000; and Newcomb, New York 12852; (518)582-2000; http://humber.northnet.org/adirondackvic

Association for the Protection of the Adirondacks (forest preserve advocacy), Schenectady, New York 12301; (518)377-1452; www.global2000.net/protectadks

Champlain Valley Heritage Network (heritage tourism promotion), Crown Point, New York 12928; (518)597-3983

Essex Community Heritage Organization (ECHO) (architectural, rural, and cultural preservation), Essex, New York 12936; (518)963-7088; www.essexny.net

Friends of the North Country (Keeseville area community preservation and improvement), Keeseville, New York 12944; (518)834-9606

Lake Champlain Basin Program (developing a management program to protect and enhance the environmental integrity and the social and economic benefits of Lake Champlain and its watershed), Grand Isle, Vermont 05458; (802)372-3213; www.lcbp.org

Lake Champlain Visitors Center (everything visitors need to know about the eastern Adirondacks and Vermont's Champlain Valley), Crown Point, New York 12928; (518)597-4646; www.lakechamplainregion.com

Lake George Association (protection, conservation, and improvement of the beauty and quality of the Lake George basin), Lake George, New York 12845; (518)668-3558; www.lakegeorgeassociation.org

Lake George Land Conservancy (preserving the water quality of
Lake George through land protection in the basin), P.O. Box 1250,
Lake Shore Drive, Bolton Landing, New York 12814; (518)644-
9673; www.nature.org/newyork/lakegeorge

Natural History Museum of the Adirondacks (natural history information and interpretation), Tupper Lake, New York 12986;
(518)359-2533; www.adknature.org

New York State Department of Environmental Conservation (care,
custody, and control of the Adirondack Forest Preserve): Ray
Brook, New York 12977; (518)897-1200; and Watertown, New York
13601; (315)785-2239; www.dec.state.ny.us

Pride of Ticonderoga (community preservation and improvement),
Ticonderoga, New York 12883; (518)585-6366;
www.ambermyst.com/pride

Residents' Committee to Protect the Adirondacks (park advocacy),
North Creek, New York 12853; (518)251-4257

Six Nations Indian Museum (lives and times of the Iroquois Nation),
Onchiota, New York 12989; (518)891-0769

bibliography

BOOKS AND REPORTS

Adirondack Regional Tourism Council. *Adirondack Waterways* and *Adirondack Great Walks and Day Hikes*, West Chazy, N.Y.: Adirondack Regional Tourism Council, 2000.

Barnett, Lincoln. *The Ancient Adirondacks*. New York: Time-Life Books, 1974.

Berry, Wendell. *Home Economics*. San Francisco: North Point Press, 1987.

Bernstein, Burton. *The Sticks: A Profile of Essex County, New York*. New York: Dodd, Mead & Co., 1971.

Brown, Eleanor. *The Forest Preserve*. Glens Falls, N.Y.: Adirondack Mountain Club, 1986.

Brown, Kenneth, and Michael Mendrick. *The Adirondacks* (Insiders Guide to). Plattsburgh, N.Y.: Press-Republican, 1997.

Colvin, Verplanck. Topographical Survey, Adirondack Region, New York, Third to Seventh Reports. Albany: Weed, Parsons & Co., 1880.

Commission on the Adirondacks in the Twenty-first Century. *The Adirondack Park in the Twenty-first Century*. Albany: State of New York, 1990.

Davis, George D., and Barbara McMartin. *2020 Vision: Fulfilling the Promise of the Adirondack Park.* Elizabethtown, N.Y.: Adirondack Council, 1988, 1990, and 1992.

DiNunzio, Michael G. *Adirondack Wildguide.* Elizabethtown, N.Y.: Adirondack Nature Conservancy and Adirondack Council, 1984.

———. *A Gift of Wildness: The Bob Marshall Great Wilderness.* Elizabethtown, N.Y.: Adirondack Council, 1992.

Doctorow, E. L. *Loon Lake.* New York: Random House, 1980.

Donaldson, Alfred L. *A History of the Adirondacks.* Harrison, N.Y.: Harbor Hill Books, 1977 (reprint of the 1921 edition published by Century Co., New York).

Farb, Nathan. *The Adirondacks.* New York: Rizzoli International Publications, 1985.

Folwell, Elizabeth. *The Adirondack Book: A Complete Guide.* Stockbridge, Mass.: Berkshire House Publishers, 1992.

Glover, James M. *A Wilderness Original: The Life of Bob Marshall.* Seattle: Mountaineers, 1986.

Goodwin, Tony (editor). *Guide to Adirondack Trails.* Lake George, N.Y.: Adirondack Mountain Club, 1993. The Mountain Club offers trail guides to all corners of the Adirondack Park.

Gould, Jim. *Rooted in Rock: New Adirondack Writing, 1975–2000.* Blue Mountain Lake, N.Y.: Adirondack Museum, 2001.

Graham, Frank, Jr. *The Adirondack Park.* New York: Alfred A. Knopf, 1978.

Hammond, Samuel H. *Wild Northern Scenes; or, Sporting Adventures with the Rifle and the Rod.* Harrison, N.Y.: Harbor Hill Books, 1979 (reprint of the 1857 edition published by Derby & Jackson, New York).

Hay, John. *The Undiscovered Country.* New York: W. W. Norton Co., 1984.

Headley, Joel T. *The Adirondack; or, Life in the Woods.* Harrison, N.Y.:

Harbor Hill Books, 1982 (reprint of the 1849 edition published by Scribner, Armstrong, New York).

Heilman, Carl E., II. *Adirondacks: Views of an American Wilderness.* New York: Rizzoli International, 1999.

Jamieson, Paul. *Adirondack Canoe Waters: North Flow.* Glens Falls, N.Y.: Adirondack Mountain Club, 1975, 1981, 1988.

———. *Adirondack Pilgrimage.* Glens Falls, N.Y.: Adirondack Mountain Club, 1986.

———. *The Adirondack Reader,* 2nd edition. Glens Falls, N.Y.: Adirondack Mountain Club, 1982.

Kaiser, Harvey H. *Great Camps of the Adirondacks.* Boston: David R. Godine, 1982.

Keller, Jane Eblen. *Adirondack Wilderness: Story of Man and Nature.* Syracuse: Syracuse University Press, 1980.

Leopold, Aldo. *The Round River: From the Journals of Aldo Leopold.* London: Oxford University Press, 1972.

Longstreth, Morris T. *The Adirondacks.* New York: Century Co., 1917.

Marsh, George Perkins. *Man and Nature.* Cambridge: Belkamp Press of Harvard University Press, 1965 (originally published by Charles Scribner in 1864).

McKibben, Bill. *The End of Nature.* New York: Random House, 1989.

McMartin, Barbara. Discover the Adirondacks Series. Woodstock, Vt.: Backcountry Publications, 1980s.

Merriam, Clinton Hart. *The Mammals of the Adirondack Region.* New York: Armo Press, 1974 (reprint of the 1884 edition published by the Press of L. S. Foster, New York).

Murray, William H. H. *Adventures in the Wilderness.* Syracuse: Syracuse University Press and Adirondack Museum, 1970 (reprint of the 1869 edition published by Fields, Osgood, & Co., Boston).

Nash, Roderick. *Wilderness and the American Mind.* New Haven: Yale University Press, 1967.

Page, Daniel H. *Sacred Life: A North American Indian Ethnohistory, Emphasizing the Iroquoians of the Eastern Woodlands.* Montreal: Pine Tree Press, 1987.

Proskine, Alec. *Adirondack Canoe Waters: South and West Flow, 2nd edition.* Glens Falls, N.Y.: Adirondack Mountain Club, 1989.

Rikhoff, Jean. *Buttes Landing.* New York: Dial Press, 1973.

Saunders, D. Andrew. *Adirondack Mammals.* Syracuse: State University of New York College of Environmental Science & Forestry, 1989.

Schaefer, Paul. *Defending the Wilderness.* Syracuse: Syracuse University Press, 1989.

————. *The Living Wilderness.* Washington, D.C.: Wilderness Society, 1965.

Schneider, Paul. *The Adirondacks: A History of America's First Wilderness.* New York: Henry Holt & Co., 1997.

Sears, George W. (pen name Nessmuk). *Woodcraft and Camping.* New York: Forest & Stream Publishing Co., 1920. Dover paperback edition, 1963.

Sylvester, Nathaniel B. *Northern New York and the Adirondack Wilderness.* Harrison, N.Y.: Harbor Hill Books, 1973 (originally published by William H. Young, Troy, N.Y., 1877).

Temporary Study Commission on the Future of the Adirondacks. *The Future of the Adirondack Park.* Albany: State of New York, 1970.

Terrie, Philip. *Contested Terrain.* Syracuse: Syracuse University Press, 1997.

Udall, Stuart. *The Quiet Crisis.* Austin, Tex.: Holt, Reinhart, & Winston, 1963.

VanValkenburgh, Norman J. *The Adirondack Forest Preserve.* Blue Mountain Lake, N.Y.: Adirondack Museum, 1979.

————. *The Forest Preserve of New York State in the Adirondack and Catskill Mountains: A Short History.* Schenectady: Adirondack Research Center, 1983.

Wallace, Paul A. *The White Roots of Peace.* Saranac Lake, N.Y.: Chauncy Press, 1986 (originally published by University of Pennsylvania Press, 1946).

Weston, Harold. *Freedom in the Wilds.* St. Huberts, N.Y.: Adirondack Trail Improvement Society, 1971.

White, William Chapman. *Adirondack Country.* Boston: Little, Brown & Co., 1954.

PERIODICALS

Adirondack Council Newsletter, Elizabethtown, N.Y. 12932. All matters environmental and others critical to both the Adirondack Park and the Adirondack Forest Preserve. Quarterly.

Adirondack Explorer, Saranac Lake, N.Y. 12983. Adventuring in and advocating for the Adirondack Park. Monthly.

Adirondack Journal of Environmental Studies, Paul Smiths, N.Y. 12970. Scientific matters presented in understandable, lay terms. Semiannually.

Adirondack Life, Jay, N.Y. 12941. All things Adirondack. Bimonthly.

Casin' the Basin, Grand Isle, Vt. 05458. All matters related to the Lake Champlain Basin, which includes 25 percent of the land and water area of the Adirondack Park. Quarterly.

The Conservationist, Albany, N.Y. 12233. Conservation matters and issues across New York State. Bimonthly.

Lake George Mirror, Lake George, N.Y. 12845. Current issues and other matters relating to Lake George. Weekly during the clement weather months.

The Northern Forest Forum, Lancaster, N.H. 03584. Forest and forestry issues relating to northern New England and the Tug Hill and Adirondack regions of New York State. Six times per year.

Wild Earth, Richmond, Vt. 05477. A melding of conservation biology and wilderness advocacy. Quarterly.

acknowledgments

There are many good books on the Adirondacks. Several are referenced here. Several picture books have been previously published. But this book is different. Look at the photos. I hope they speak to you of someone who, like few others, knows, understands, respects, and loves this enormous park and wants, through photography, to enlist your emotions and earn your support for land stewardship and preservation. Reviewers have noted that this is the first time one book has told the full story of the Adirondack Park, combined with artful, stunning photography.

I took my first photograph at age twenty-two, moments after my mother (thank you, Alice Randorf) had given me an $8.00 Kodak Brownie Starflash camera for graduation from college. The photo was of a toy boat, shot through a stand of cattails on our farm pond. A couple of years later I entered it in a First Army photo contest at Fort Dix, and it won honorable mention. From that day forward my eyes were hanging out, always on the lookout for exciting images. Later I was to live in California and then Hawaii, in short order. I got myself a good 35mm single lens reflex camera. I stalked the surrounding landscapes like a hunter after game.

Nowhere have the "hunting" opportunities been greater than in the

Adirondacks. The size, diversity, and uniqueness of the place ensure that I will never run out of subjects to photograph.

I ESPECIALLY THANK the Adirondack Council and the Adirondack Park Agency for sending me into the Adirondack woods with my camera, while continuing to provide me with paychecks. For their support and encouragement, I will be eternally grateful.

I give special thanks also to Pat Randorf, Anne Lacy, and Jennifer Knapp for accompanying me along countless miles of trail and waterways into the Adirondack back country, where a number of photos were taken, and for their patience while I waited for the right light or for the wildflower to stand still.

Special thanks are also due Timothy Barnett, Robin Pell, Duncan and Fran Elder, Ralph Friedman, Sue Cullman, Dorothy C. Treisman, Arthur Crocker, Bill and BizAnne Hord, Frances Beinecke, Harold and Lyn Jerry, Kim Elliman, Peter Sanders, John and Margot Ernst, Steve and Ellen Scholle, Barbara Glaser, Katharine Preston, Sally Johnson, and all the others who made it possible for me to see corners of the Adirondacks to which I might not otherwise have found my way.

Michael DiNunzio, Clarence Petty, and John Sheehan read the manuscript closely for accuracy, which was a great help. Bill McKibben kindly agreed to pen the foreword.

Thanks also to Clarence Petty, Greenleaf Chase, and Paul Schaefer for the inspiration their friendship and long-term love and understanding of the Adirondacks have provided me and for leading me to the riches of the Adirondack wilderness.

I'd like to express appreciation to Margy Holden for her editorial assistance and to Jackie Audino for typing, typing, and retyping. And to Anne Trachtenberg for her fine copy editing, which was desperately needed. Linda Forlifer, senior manuscript editor at JHU Press, further refined the text. Elaine Burke also did a lot of typing and retyping and put the manuscript on the computer. George F. Thompson, president,

Charles E. Little, vice president, and Dick Beamish, a founding director of the Center for American Places, provided much encouragement, as did John Davis and George Davis. Atea Ring made some final corrections.

Last but not least, the Adirondack Council elected to endow the book to the level of $30,000 or more, thus becoming the book's prime sponsor and ensuring a high-quality publication at an affordable price. Furthermore, a program of the J. M. Kaplan Fund, the Nordlys Foundation, and the Norcross Wildlife Foundation, Inc., generously assisted the council in raising these funds.

193

Gary Alvin Randorf—environmentalist, naturalist, writer, photographer—is senior counselor for the Adirondack Council in Elizabethtown, New York, an organization that he directed for eleven years. He has also worked as a planner, writer, and photographer for the Adirondack Park Agency. A resident of the Adirondack Park for thirty years, his photographs and words have been published in a number of periodicals and books.

Other Photography Books in the Series

Andrew Borowiec
Along the Ohio

Laurie Brown, with poetry by Martha Ronk
and a concluding essay by Charles E. Little
Recent Terrains: Terraforming the American West

Terry Evans, with an introductory essay by Tony Hiss
Disarming the Prairie

Frank Gohlke, with a concluding essay by John C. Hudson
Measure of Emptiness: Grain Elevators in the American Landscape

Peter Goin
Nuclear Landscapes

Stanley Greenberg, with an
introductory essay by Thomas H. Garver
Invisible New York: The Hidden Infrastructure of the City

Richard Misrach, with Myriam Weisang Misrach
Bravo 20: The Bombing of the American West

Eric L. Paddock
Belonging to the West

Michael Putnam, with an introduction by Robert Sklar
*Silent Screens: The Decline and Transformation of
the American Movie Theater*